VIRGIL
AENEID I

VIRGIL

AENEID
BOOK I

Edited with Introduction,
Notes and Vocabulary by

H.E. Gould & J.L. Whiteley

Bristol Classical Press

This impression 2003
This edition published in 1984 by
Bristol Classical Press
an imprint of
Gerald Duckworth & Co. Ltd.
61 Frith Street, London W1D 3JL
Tel: 020 7434 4242
Fax: 020 7434 4420
inquiries@duckworth-publishers.co.uk
www.ducknet.co.uk

First published in 1946 by Macmillan Education Ltd

A catalogue record for this book is available
from the British Library

ISBN 0 86292 167 8

Cover illustration: Virgil from the Ara Pietatis Augustae of
Claudian date (41–54 AD), Villa Medici, Rome
(drawing by Jean Bees).

Printed and bound in Great Britain by
Antony Rowe Ltd, Eastbourne

CONTENTS

LIST OF ILLUSTRATIONS

FOREWORD

THIS edition of Vergil's Aeneid I has been prepared on the same principles as previous volumes in the Modern School Classics. That is to say, the editors, believing that the annotated classical texts of the past generation give too little practical help in translation, and yet at the same time have their commentaries overloaded with unnecessary information on points only remotely connected with the text, have sought to write notes that will make it possible for the school boy or girl of today, who is quite likely to begin the preparation of the School Certificate set books without having previously read any continuous Latin texts at all, to produce, in reasonable time, and without the discouragement of being baffled by difficulties, a correct translation of passages set by their teachers for preparation.

In these times such pupils will need a great deal of help which in the spacious days of classical teaching fifty years ago they were considered not to require, and they will need moreover that such help should at first be given repeatedly, until each difficulty of construction becomes familiar.

The editors, bearing in mind, as they have tried to do throughout, the difficulties experienced by present-day pupils in the study of a subject which once received a much more generous share of the time-table, hope that they have done something, in the present edition, to smooth their path.

H. E. G.
J. L. W.

LONDON, 1946.

INTRODUCTION

Publius Vergilius Maro

VERGIL was born on 15th October, 70 B.C. at Andes near Mantua in Cisalpine Gaul—the Lombardy plain. Andes is usually identified with the present Pietole, three miles from Mantua ; this identification, however, has been rejected by some modern scholars, who favour a site close to the existing towns of Carpendolo and Calvisano.

The poet's family seems to have been of some local importance, and his father, who owned and worked a farm, was able to give his son the ancient equivalent of a university education. Vergil studied at Cremona and Milan, and later went to Rome to complete his course in rhetoric and philosophy.

No doubt his father wished Vergil to make his way, as Cicero had done, by his eloquence, first in the law courts as a pleader, or barrister, and then in politics by standing as a candidate for the various magistracies which led ultimately to the consulship and a seat in the senate. Vergil's temperament, however, for he was shy, nervous, and awkward in society, was quite unsuited to such a career, and after a single appearance before a jury, he decided to devote his life to philosophy and poetry.

Vergil returned to his native district, where he began to write his first important work, the Eclogues, or

ix

Bucolics, ten poems, in semi-dramatic form, in which the persons are imaginary shepherds and their loves. This fashion of poetry, called ' pastoral ', was developed by the Sicilian Greek Theocritus. The Eclogues made Vergil's reputation as a poet and gained the attention of Maecenas, who at that time was the most trusted adviser in home affairs of Octavian, heir and successor of Julius Caesar, and destined shortly to become master of the Greco-Roman world as the first Roman Emperor, Augustus.

During this period of his life, in 41 B.C., Vergil was one of the many landed proprietors who saw their farms ruthlessly confiscated and allotted to demobilized soldiers—a common event during those troubled years of civil war which preceded the collapse of the Roman Republic. Fortunately for the poet, however, the fame of the Eclogues and his friendship with Maecenas made Vergil's position secure under the new regime, and enabled him to devote the rest of his life to poetical composition, free from all economic anxiety, at Naples and Nola in Campania.

Thus, in or about 37 B.C., Vergil began his second great work, the Georgics, a long poem, in four books, which describes the Roman methods of farming, the production of crops, of the vine and the olive, the breeding of stock and the keeping of bees. As we know from Vergil himself that he was asked to write on this subject by Maecenas, we may safely assume that this poem was designed as propaganda for Augustus' ' new order ' in Italy, and to reinforce that Emperor's attempts to revive Roman religion, Roman agriculture, and the simple but hardy virtues which had made Rome great.

The two thousand odd lines of the poem were written very slowly, the years 37–30 B.C. being devoted to their composition, and reveal the highest standard of pure craftsmanship yet reached in Latin Poetry. Moreover, though his subject in this poem might seem unlikely to produce great poetry, Vergil found the theme so congenial to his nature that he overcame the many difficulties, and not only produced a valuable text-book for farmers, but also wrote some of the noblest poetry in the Latin language.

Soon after the completion of the Georgics, Vergil, now forty years of age, embarked, again no doubt at the instigation of his political patrons, upon his greatest and most ambitious work, the writing of an epic, i.e. heroic narrative poem, the Aeneid, which should rival Homer's Iliad and Odyssey, and honour the imperial achievements of the Roman race, glorify the Roman character and focus Roman national sentiment on Augustus as the man sent by destiny to bring peace, stability, and prosperity to the Greco-Roman world, which had been racked for so many years by civil war, fear, and uncertainty.

The Aeneid occupied Vergil's whole attention for the remaining years of his life. In 19 B.C., after a journey to the East, he fell ill on his return to Italy at Brundisium. His health had never been robust, and realizing that his end was near he gave instructions that the great epic, for which he had planned a three years' revision, and of whose imperfections, as an intensely self-critical artist, he was very conscious, should be destroyed. This instruction, fortunately for literature, was disregarded by the poet's literary executors.

The Aeneid is an epic poem in twelve books, and tells how a Trojan prince, Aeneas, a survivor from the sack of Troy by the Greeks, is directed by the gods to seek a new home in Italy. In that land, after many vicissitudes, he settles with his Trojan companions, and it is from these colonists that the Romans liked to believe that they were sprung. Into this legend, Vergil weaves a glorification of the family of Augustus, connecting the Julian clan, to which it belonged, with Iulus, the son of Aeneas.

Criticism of the poem has always recognized its superlative artistry, despite Vergil's own dissatisfaction with its lack of final polish, and is unanimous in detecting in Vergil's mind, and reflected by the poem, a profound sensitivity and sympathy with human troubles, which are hardly paralleled in Latin literature. In so far as judgment has been adverse, it has fastened on the character of the hero, Aeneas himself, in whom the virtue of *pietas*, ' dutifulness ', whether towards father, country or gods, is allowed prominence at the expense of warmer and more human feelings.

The story of the epic, book by book, is as follows :

Book I. Aeneas and his companions are driven by a storm aroused by Juno, implacable enemy of the Trojan race, towards the North African coast, where, thanks to the intervention of Neptune, most of the ships find shelter, their crews landing safely and making their way to Carthage. In this city, which has just been founded by Dido, a young widowed princess from Tyre, they are hospitably received by the queen, who, at a banquet, invites Aeneas to relate the story of his wanderings.

BOOK II. The Trojan hero begins his narrative with the story of the final siege, capture, and sack of Troy. We hear of the treacherous Sinon, who feigns to be a deserter, persecuted by his Greek fellows, in order to gain entrance to the city, of the trick of the Wooden Horse, the cruel death of Laocoon and his sons, who sought to warn the Trojans of their approaching doom, the entry of the Greeks, their murder of King Priam, and the escape of Aeneas from the burning city with his aged father, Anchises, his young son, Iulus, known also as Ascanius, and the household gods. In the confusion his wife Creusa is lost, but later Aeneas meets her ghost and is told that he is destined to found a new kingdom in Italy.

BOOK III. The narrative continues with the escape of Aeneas and his Trojan comrades from the mainland, and their voyage to various places in search of the ' promised land '—to Thrace, Delos, Crete, and finally to the West, by way of the Strophades Islands, and the coast of Epirus (Albania), where Aeneas is advised by Helenus to sail round Sicily, to make for the west coast of Italy, and there to consult a prophetess, the Sibyl, at Cumae, and to appease Juno. Aeneas does as Helenus suggests, and thus, after seven years' wandering over the Eastern Mediterranean, he arrives at the western end of Sicily, where he spends the winter. Aeneas concludes his narrative to the queen, his hostess, by recording the death in Sicily of his father, Anchises.

BOOK IV. Meanwhile Dido, who has been greatly attracted to Aeneas from the first owing to the influence of Venus, his mother, now falls more and more deeply in love with him. Shortly after his arrival at Carthage, by the power of Juno and Venus, who from quite different motives favour such a development, Dido and Aeneas become lovers. Jupiter, however, now intervenes, and warns Aeneas, through Mercury, that he must leave Africa at once and fulfil his destined task of founding a new realm in Italy. Realizing the strength of Dido's passion for him, he tries to depart secretly, but his intentions become known to her. Yet he remains unmoved by her entreaties, which turn in the end to words of scorn and hatred. As he sails away, Dido destroys herself.

BOOK V. Aeneas returns to western Sicily and there celebrates the anniversary of his father's death with funeral games.[1] During the latter, Juno, pursuing her relentless hostility to their race, persuades the Trojan women, weary as they are of their wanderings, to set fire to the ships, but a sudden rain-storm subdues the flames

[1] The elaborate account of these games, which occupies most of Book V, is no doubt due to the influence of Homer, who in the Iliad describes at great length the funeral games of the hero Patroclus.

and only four are destroyed. The Trojans sail away from Sicily. On the voyage, Palinurus, the helmsman, is overcome by sleep, and falling overboard, is drowned.

BOOK VI. In this, to many readers the finest book of the poem, Aeneas, having at last set foot on the coast of western Italy, visits the Sibyl of Cumae and receives from her directions for the visit he longs to pay to the underworld. Armed with the ' golden bough ', which alone can procure him access to the nether regions of Hades, he traverses the various quarters of that kingdom, and meets the spirit of his father, who parades for Aeneas the souls of all great Romans that are awaiting incarnation.[1] In this way Vergil is able to give his readers a kind of national cavalcade of all the great figures in Roman history from the earliest times down to his own day. Thus the pageant closes with the greatest figure of them all, the emperor Augustus.

The sixth book contains the famous lines (851–3), which epitomize the Roman's pride in the city's greatness as an imperial power :

> Tu regere imperio populos, Romane, memento;
> Hae tibi erunt artes ; pacisque imponere morem,
> Parcere subiectis, et debellare superbos.

' Thou, O Roman, remember to rule the nations 'neath thy sway,
These shall be thine arts, to impose the laws of peace,
To spare the conquered and to chasten the proud in war.'

[1] Note again Vergil's indebtedness to Homer. Odysseus, too, in Book XI of the Odyssey, is made to visit the underworld.

BOOK VII. Aeneas at last enters his promised land by the mouth of the river Tiber, the natural frontier between the districts of Latium, lying south of the river, and Etruria to the north. He is welcomed by Latinus, king of Latium, who sees in Aeneas the bridegroom for his daughter, Lavinia, for whom he has been advised by an oracle to find a foreign husband.

Turnus, however, chieftain of the neighbouring Rutuli, and worthiest of Lavinia's suitors, is enraged at the proposal of Latinus, and, supported by Amata, the latter's queen, arouses the Latins against the Trojans. The book closes with a magnificent catalogue of the Italian forces—another epic convention, originating in Homer's catalogue of the Greek ships in the Iliad, Book II.

BOOK VIII. The river god Tiberinus sends Aeneas to seek aid from a Greek, Evander, who has settled on the Palatine Hill in what is destined to be the future Rome. Evander promises help and conducts Aeneas through the city, explaining the origin of various Roman sites and names. Venus persuades Vulcan, her husband, to make Aeneas a suit of armour and a shield,[1] on which are depicted in relief various events in the future history of Rome, down to the battle of Actium, 31 B.C., by which Vergil's patron Augustus gained undisputed sovereignty over the ancient world.

BOOK IX. While Aeneas is absent, Turnus makes an attempt, barely frustrated, to storm the Trojan camp

[1] Homer, too, in the Iliad, Book XVIII, describes at length a shield, that of the Greek hero, Achilles.

by the Tiber, and is successful in setting fire to their ships. Nisus and Euryalus, two Trojans, endeavour to slip through the enemy lines in order to inform Aeneas of the critical situation. They slay some of the foe, but are eventually discovered and killed. The next day, when Turnus renews his assault, he succeeds in entering the camp, but is cut off, and only effects his escape by plunging into the Tiber.

BOOK X. A council of the gods is held in Olympus and Jupiter decides to leave the issue of the war to fate. Aeneas now wins the support of an Etruscan army which has revolted against the cruelties of the king Mezentius, and joined by reinforcements from Evander under the leadership of the latter's son, Pallas, he returns to aid the hard-pressed Trojans. In the furious fighting, Mezentius and his son Lausus are slain, but Turnus kills Pallas.

BOOK XI. A truce is arranged for the burial of the dead. On the arrival of an embassy from the Latins, Aeneas offers to settle the issue with a single combat between himself and Turnus. The Latins hold a council of war and determine to continue the struggle, but they are defeated a second time by the Trojans and their allies in spite of many deeds of valour, especially on the part of Camilla, a warrior maiden who is killed in the fighting.

BOOK XII. Another truce is arranged, and Turnus agrees to accept Aeneas' challenge, despite the opposition of the queen Amata and his sister, Juturna. The latter provokes the Latins to violate the truce. In the ensuing struggle Aeneas is wounded, but is miraculously healed by his mother, the goddess Venus. He returns to the fray, routs the Latins and Rutulians and eventually meets Turnus in single combat. The Rutulian chieftain is wounded and rendered helpless. Aeneas is minded to spare him until he notices that he is wearing the belt of the dead Pallas, whereupon he slays him.

The Metre of the Poem

Most English verse consists of lines in which stressed syllables alternate with unstressed, as, for example in the lines :

' The ploughman homeward plods his weary way,

And leaves the world to darkness and to me.

Such verse is called *accentual*.

The principle of Greek and Latin verse is different. It is based on the rhythmical arrangement of long and short syllables, the long syllables taking twice as long to pronounce as the short. This system may be compared with music, long syllables corresponding to *crotchets* and short to *quavers*, one *crotchet* being equal to two *quavers*. This type of verse is called *quantitative*.

Just as, to appreciate the rhythm of English verse, you are taught to *scan*, i.e. to divide the lines into *feet* and mark the stress in each foot, so you must learn to scan Latin verse by a similar division into feet and by marking the syllables long (–) or short (⌣). Not only is it necessary to do this in order to understand the construction of the verse and the musical qualities of the poetry, but the ability to do so is a great help in translation, by making it possible to distinguish words alike in spelling but different in quantity, for example, *pŏpŭlŭs*, ' people ', from *pōpŭlŭs*, ' poplar tree '.

The verses of the Aeneid are called heroic hexameters. In this verse two kinds of feet, or bars, are found. One is the *dactyl*, a long syllable followed by two short syllables, the other, the *spondee*, two long syllables. Each line, or hexameter, contains six feet, the first four of which may be either dactyls, or spondees, the fifth being almost always a dactyl and the sixth a spondee. In place of this sixth-foot spondee a trochee (– ⌣) is allowable.

Thus the scheme of the hexameter is as follows :

1	2	3	4	5	6
– ⌣ ⌣	– ⌣ ⌣	– ⌣ ⌣	– ⌣ ⌣	– ⌣ ⌣	– –
– –	– –	– –	– –		– ⌣

or (at left, spanning both rows)

In the scansion of these lines, no account is taken of syllables at the close of words *ending* in a vowel or an *m*, if they are followed immediately by a word *commencing* with a vowel or an *h*. Such a final syllable is said to be *elided*, ' struck out ', though it was more probably slurred in pronunciation. Thus in l. 3 of the present book,

Litora multum ille et terris iactatus et alto,

the *-um* of *multum* and the final *-e* of *ille* are ignored in scanning.

*   *   *

A long syllable is one that contains a vowel long *by nature*, or a diphthong ; or a vowel, naturally short, that is long *by position*, i.e., is followed by two consonants.

A short syllable is one that contains a vowel short *by nature* and ends either with no consonant, or with only one.

The two consonants which have been mentioned as having the effect of lengthening a syllable need not both occur in the same word. Thus in l. 3, *et* is long, though the *e* in *et* is naturally short, because that *e* is followed by a *t* and the *t* of *terris*.

PROSODY

The following information about the quantity of Latin syllables will be found useful.

A. Relating to all syllables.

All diphthongs are long, except before another vowel.

B. Relating to final syllables.

1. Final *a* is usually short.

Except

(*a*) in the abl. sg. of 1st decl. nouns, e.g. *mensā* ;

(*b*) in the 2nd sg. imperative active of 1st conjugation verbs, e.g. *amā* ;

(*c*) in indeclinable words such as *intereā, frustrā*.

2. Final *e* is usually short.

Except

(*a*) in the abl. sg. of 5th decl. nouns, e.g. *aciĕ* ;

(*b*) in the 2nd sg. imperative active of 2nd conjugation verbs, e.g. *monē* ;

(*c*) in adverbs formed from adjectives of the 1st
and 2nd declensions, e.g. *pulchrē*, from *pulcher,
-chra, -chrum*. (Note, however, *benĕ, malĕ*.)

3. Final *i* is usually long.

Except in *mihi, tibi, sibi, ubi, ibi*, in which it may be
long or short, and in *quasi, nisi*.

4. Final *o* is usually long.

Except in *modo, duo, ego*.

C. Final syllables of words of more than one syllable,
ending in any single consonant other than *s*, are
short.

Except

(*a*) *dispār* ;

(*b*) in the perfects *iīt* and *petiīt*.

D. 1. Final *as, os, es*, are long.

Except

(*a*) *compŏs, penĕs* ;

(*b*) in nominatives singular in *es* of 3rd declension
nouns (consonant stems) having genitive singular
in *-ĕtis, -ĭtis, -idis* ; e.g. *segĕs, milĕs, obsĕs*.
(But note *pariēs, abiēs*.)

(*c*) In compounds of *es* (from *sum*), e.g. *abĕs,
prodĕs*.

2. Final *us* and *is* are short.

Except *ūs*

    (*a*) in gen. sg., nom., voc. and acc. pl. of 4th decl. nouns, e.g. *gradūs* ;

    (*b*) in the nom. sg. of consonant stem 3rd decl. nouns having gen. sg. with a long syllable before the last, e.g. *tellūs* (*-ūris*), *palūs* (*-ūdis*), *virtūs* (*-ūtis*).

And except *īs*

    (*c*) in dat. and abl. pl., e.g. *mensīs, dominīs, vinīs* ;

    (*d*) in acc. pl. of 3rd decl. *-i* stems, e.g. *navīs, omnīs* ;

    (*e*) in the 2nd pers. sg. of 4th conjugation verbs, e.g. *audīs* ; and in *sīs*, and compounds of *sīs*, as *possīs* ; and in *velīs, nolīs, malīs*, and *īs* (from *eo*).

E. Quantity of syllables determined by position in the same word.

1. A syllable ending with a vowel or diphthong, immediately followed by a syllable beginning with a vowel, or with *h* and a vowel, is short ; e.g. *vĭa, prăeustus, trăhit*.

Except

    (*a*) in the case of genitives in *-ius*, e.g. *alīus, solīus, utrīus*. (But note *illĭus*.)

    (*b*) *e* preceding *i* in 5th decl. nouns, e.g. *diēi* and *ēi* (from *is*).

(c) the syllable *fī* in *fīo*.   (But note *fieri*, *fierem*,
the *i* being short before *er*.)

2. A syllable containing a vowel immediately followed
by two consonants, or by *x* or *z*, which are really double
consonants (*cs* and *ds*) is long ; e.g. the second syllable
in *regent, auspex*.

Except if the two consonants are a combination of
one of the following, *b, c, d, f, g, p, t*, with (following)
l or *r*.

If a short vowel precedes such a combination the
syllable is not necessarily long.

Finally it must be remembered that these rules apply
to Latin words only, and not to many Greek proper
names which will be encountered in this book.

*   *   *

Let us see now if, with the information given above,
we can scan one of the hexameters of this poem.

Looking at line 35, for example,

Vela dabant laeti et spumas salis aere ruebant,

(i) see first whether any syllable requires to be
elided, i.e. not taken into account. In this line the
final *i* of *laeti* will be disregarded before the vowel *e* of
et.

(ii) Mark long (–) all syllables where long quantity
can be determined by the rules given above.

bant, et, mas, bant

are all long syllables (by rule E. 2).

ae (*laeti*) and *ae* (*aere*) are long syllables because they are diphthongs (Rule A).

This now gives us

Vela dabānt lāet(ī) et spumās salis āere ruebānt.

(iii) Mark short (◡) all syllables whose short quantity can be determined by rule.

The *a* of *vela*, the *is* of *salis*, and the *e* of *aere* are short—Rules B 1, B 2 and D 2, respectively.

Thus we now have

Velă dabānt lāet(ī) et spumās salĭs āerĕ ruebānt.

Generally speaking, it will be found that such an application of the rules of prosody will give enough syllables of known quantity to make it possible to scan the line completely.

To do this, work backwards from the end of the line, because the pattern of the last two feet

(– ◡ ◡ | – – or – ◡) is constant.

This gives us for these feet [1]

āerĕ rŭ | ēbānt.

Working backwards again, the fourth foot is a dactyl, the third a spondee, the second a spondee, and

[1] Very occasionally a spondee is found in the 5th foot. See l. 617 and the note in this book.

the first a dactyl. Thus the whole line, divided into feet and with the quantities marked, is :

$$V\bar{e}l\breve{a}\ d\breve{a}\ |\ b\bar{a}nt\ l\bar{a}e\ |\ t(\bar{\bar{i}})\ \bar{e}t\ sp\bar{u}\ |\ m\bar{a}s\ s\breve{a}l\breve{i}s\ |\ \bar{a}e\breve{r}e\ r\breve{u}\ |\ \bar{e}b\bar{a}nt.$$

One thing remains to be done before the scansion is complete. It is a rule that, usually in the third foot, more rarely in the fourth, one word must end and another begin. This is called caesura or ' cutting '. If the break occurs after the first syllable of the foot, the caesura is said to be strong ; if, after the second, weak. In this line, we obviously have a strong caesura in the third foot. The caesura is regularly marked in scansion by a pair of vertical lines.

Thus the scansion of the line, as completed, is

$$\begin{array}{cccccc} \text{I} & 2 & 3 & 4 & 5 & 6 \end{array}$$
$$V\bar{e}l\breve{a}\ d\breve{a}\ |\ b\bar{a}nt\ l\bar{a}e\ |\ t(\bar{\bar{i}})\ \bar{e}t\ \|\ sp\bar{u}\ |\ m\bar{a}s\ s\breve{a}l\breve{i}s\ |\ \bar{a}e\breve{r}e\ r\breve{u}\ |\ \bar{e}b\bar{a}nt.$$

You will find that with careful attention to the pronunciation of Latin words, you will gradually learn to scan by ear, without the necessity of applying for help to the rules of prosody. You should try to develop this power as early as possible.

Note that the scheme of the hexameter makes it elastic, and gives it variable length, as long as 17 or as short as 13 syllables. This makes possible such onomatopoeic lines as

$$Qu\bar{a}dr\breve{u}p\breve{e}\text{-}\ |\ d\bar{a}nt\breve{e}\ p\breve{u}\text{-}\ |\ tr\bar{e}m\ s\breve{o}n\breve{i}\text{-}\ |\ t\bar{u}\ qu\breve{a}t\breve{i}t\ |\ \bar{u}ng\breve{u}l\breve{a}$$
$$c\bar{a}mp\breve{u}m$$

(where the poet, describing the galloping of horses, imitates the sound of them), and as

$$\bar{\imath}ll\bar{(\imath)}\ \bar{\imath}n\text{-} \mid \bar{te}r\ \bar{se}\text{-} \mid \bar{se}\ m\bar{a}g\text{-} \mid n\bar{a}\ v\bar{\imath} \mid br\bar{a}cch\breve{\imath}\breve{a} \mid t\bar{o}ll\bar{u}nt$$

(where again sound is matched to sense, for the line describes the alternate blows upon an anvil delivered by two smiths).

VERGIL

AENEID I

*' I am about to sing of the Trojan hero, Aeneas, who founded our
Roman race. Help me, Muse, to tell how Juno opposed him
in this enterprise.'*

ARMA virumque cano, Troiae qui primus ab oris
Italiam fato profugus Lavinaque venit
litora—multum ille et terris iactatus et alto
vi superum, saevae memorem Iunonis ob iram,
multa quoque et bello passus, dum conderet urbem   5
inferretque deos Latio—genus unde Latinum
Albanique patres atque altae moenia Romae.
   Musa, mihi causas memora, quo numine laeso
quidve dolens regina deum tot volvere casus
insignem pietate virum, tot adire labores   10
impulerit. tantaene animis caelestibus irae?

*Juno's love of Carthage, and the hatred she feels for the Trojans,
whose descendants are destined to overthrow that city.*

   Urbs antiqua fuit (Tyrii tenuere coloni)
Karthago, Italiam contra Tiberinaque longe
ostia, dives opum studiisque asperrima belli ;
quam Iuno fertur terris magis omnibus unam   15
posthabita coluisse Samo : hic illius arma,
hic currus fuit ; hoc regnum dea gentibus esse,

THE JUDGMENT OF PARIS.

si qua fata sinant, iam tum tenditque fovetque.
progeniem sed enim Troiano a sanguine duci
audierat, Tyrias olim quae verteret arces ;　　　20

hinc populum late regem belloque superbum
venturum excidio Libyae : sic volvere Parcas.
id metuens veterisque memor Saturnia belli,
prima quod ad Troiam pro caris gesserat Argis
(necdum etiam causae irarum saevique dolores   25
exciderant animo ; manet alta mente repostum
iudicium Paridis spretaeque iniuria formae
et genus invisum, et rapti Ganymedis honores)—

ZEUS AND GANYMEDE.

his accensa super iactatos aequore toto
Troas, reliquias Danaum atque immitis Achilli,   30
arcebat longe Latio, multosque per annos
errabant acti fatis maria omnia circum.
tantae molis erat Romanam condere gentem.

*Juno, seeing the fleet of Aeneas on its way to Italy, plans to
    scatter it, and to this end visits Aeolus, King of the
    Winds.*

Vix e conspectu Siculae telluris in altum
vela dabant laeti et spumas salis aere ruebant,   35
cum Iuno aeternum servans sub pectore vulnus
haec secum : ' mene incepto desistere victam,
nec posse Italia Teucrorum avertere regem?
quippe vetor fatis. Pallasne exurere classem
Argivum atque ipsos potuit summergere ponto   40
unius ob noxam et furias Aiacis Oilei?
ipsa Iovis rapidum iaculata e nubibus ignem,
disiecitque rates evertitque aequora ventis,
illum exspirantem transfixo pectore flammas
turbine corripuit scopuloque infixit acuto ;   45
ast ego, quae divum incedo regina Iovisque
et soror et coniunx, una cum gente tot annos
bella gero. et quisquam numen Iunonis adorat
praeterea, aut supplex aris imponet honorem?'
Talia flammato secum dea corde volutans   50
nimborum in patriam, loca feta furentibus Austris,
Aeoliam venit. hic vasto rex Aeolus antro
luctantes ventos tempestatesque sonoras

imperio premit ac vinclis et carcere frenat.
illi indignantes magno cum murmure montis 55
circum claustra fremunt ; celsa sedet Aeolus arce
sceptra tenens, mollitque animos et temperat iras :
ni faciat, maria ac terras caelumque profundum
quippe ferant rapidi secum verrantque per auras.
sed pater omnipotens speluncis abdidit atris 60
hoc metuens, molemque et montes insuper altos
imposuit, regemque dedit qui foedere certo
et premere et laxas sciret dare iussus habenas.
ad quem tum Iuno supplex his vocibus usa est :

*Juno asks Aeolus to free the winds and raise a tempest. He
agrees, and as the storm clouds gather Aeneas despairs.*

' Aeole, namque tibi divum pater atque hominum
   rex 65
et mulcere dedit fluctus et tollere vento,
gens inimica mihi Tyrrhenum navigat aequor,
Ilium in Italiam portans victosque penates :
incute vim ventis summersasque obrue puppes,
aut age diversos et disice corpora ponto. 70
sunt mihi bis septem praestanti corpore Nymphae,
quarum quae forma pulcherrima, Deiopea,
conubio iungam stabili propriamque dicabo,
omnes ut tecum meritis pro talibus annos
exigat et pulchra faciat te prole parentem.' 75
Aeolus haec contra: 'tuus, o regina, quid optes
explorare labor ; mihi iussa capessere fas est.
tu mihi quodcumque hoc regni, tu sceptra Iovemque

concilias, tu das epulis accumbere divum,
nimborumque facis tempestatumque potentem.'   80
    Haec ubi dicta, cavum conversa cuspide montem
impulit in latus : ac venti velut agmine facto,
qua data porta, ruunt et terras turbine perflant.
incubuere mari totumque a sedibus imis
una Eurusque Notusque ruunt creberque procellis   85
Africus, et vastos volvunt ad litora fluctus.
insequitur clamorque virum stridorque rudentum.
eripiunt subito nubes caelumque diemque
Teucrorum ex oculis ; ponto nox incubat atra.
intonuere poli et crebris micat ignibus aether   90
praesentemque viris intentant omnia mortem.
extemplo Aeneae solvuntur frigore membra ;
ingemit, et duplices tendens ad sidera palmas
talia voce refert : ' o terque quaterque beati,
quis ante ora patrum Troiae sub moenibus altis   95
contigit oppetere! o Danaum fortissime gentis
Tydide, mene Iliacis occumbere campis
non potuisse tuaque animam hanc effundere dextra,
saevus ubi Aeacidae telo iacet Hector, ubi ingens
Sarpedon, ubi tot Simois correpta sub undis   100
scuta virum galeasque et fortia corpora volvit? '

The havoc wrought by the tempest.

    Talia iactanti stridens Aquilone procella
velum adversa ferit, fluctusque ad sidera tollit.
franguntur remi ; tum prora avertit et undis
dat latus ; insequitur cumulo praeruptus aquae mons. 105

HECTOR'S BODY DRAGGED ROUND THE TOMB OF PATROCLUS.
Achilles is the helmeted figure behind the horses.
(See also notes, ll. 483-5).

HECTOR'S BODY RANSOMED
Achilles reclines upon a couch; the bearded figure, left, is Priam; under the couch
is the body of Hector.

hi summo in fluctu pendent, his unda dehiscens
terram inter fluctus aperit ; furit aestus harenis.
tres Notus abreptas in saxa latentia torquet
(saxa vocant Itali mediis quae in fluctibus Aras,
dorsum immane mari summo), tres Eurus ab alto   110
in brevia et syrtes urget, miserabile visu,
inliditque vadis atque aggere cingit harenae.
unam, quae Lycios fidumque vehebat Oronten,
ipsius ante oculos ingens a vertice pontus
in puppim ferit : excutitur pronusque magister   115
volvitur in caput ; ast illam ter fluctus ibidem
torquet agens circum, et rapidus vorat aequore vertex.
apparent rari nantes in gurgite vasto,
arma virum tabulaeque et Troïa gaza per undas.
iam validam Ilionei navem, iam fortis Achatae,   120
et qua vectus Abas, et qua grandaevus Aletes,
vicit hiems ; laxis laterum compagibus omnes
accipiunt inimicum imbrem rimisque fatiscunt.

*Neptune, roused by the roaring of the elements, rebukes the winds
and allays the tempest.*

Interea magno misceri murmure pontum
emissamque hiemem sensit Neptunus et imis   125
stagna refusa vadis, graviter commotus ; et alto
prospiciens summa placidum caput extulit unda.
disiectam Aeneae toto videt aequore classem,
fluctibus oppressos Troas caelique ruina.
nec latuere doli fratrem Iunonis et irae.   130
Eurum ad se Zephyrumque vocat, dehinc talia fatur :

' Tantane vos generis tenuit fiducia vestri?
iam caelum terramque meo sine numine, venti,
miscere et tantas audetis tollere moles?
quos ego—sed motos praestat componere fluctus.   135

NEPTUNE.

post mihi non simili poena commissa luetis.
maturate fugam, regique haec dicite vestro :
non illi imperium pelagi saevumque tridentem,
sed mihi sorte datum.   tenet ille immania saxa,
vestras, Eure, domos ; illa se iactet in aula   140
Aeolus et clauso ventorum carcere regnet.'

Sic ait, et dicto citius tumida aequora placat,
collectasque fugat nubes solemque reducit.
Cymothoë simul et Triton adnixus acuto
detrudunt naves scopulo ; levat ipse tridenti   145
et vastas aperit syrtes et temperat aequor,
atque rotis summas levibus perlabitur undas.
ac veluti magno in populo cum saepe coorta est
seditio saevitque animis ignobile vulgus,
iamque faces et saxa volant, furor arma ministrat : 150
tum pietate gravem ac meritis si forte virum quem
conspexere, silent arrectisque auribus astant ;
ille regit dictis animos et pectora mulcet :
sic cunctus pelagi cecidit fragor, aequora postquam
prospiciens genitor caeloque invectus aperto   155
flectit equos curruque volans dat lora secundo.

*Aeneas and the remnant of his fleet reach a sheltered bay on the
African coast. They restore their strength with a feast of
venison, and Aeneas heartens them with words of confidence.*

Defessi Aeneadae quae proxima litora cursu
contendunt petere, et Libyae vertuntur ad oras.
est in secessu longo locus : insula portum
efficit obiectu laterum, quibus omnis ab alto   160
frangitur inque sinus scindit sese unda reductos.
hinc atque hinc vastae rupes geminique minantur
in caelum scopuli, quorum sub vertice late
aequora tuta silent : tum silvis scaena coruscis
desuper, horrentique atrum nemus imminet umbra ; 165
fronte sub adversa scopulis pendentibus antrum,

intus aquae dulces vivoque sedilia saxo,
nympharum domus. hic fessas non vincula naves
ulla tenent, unco non alligat ancora morsu.
huc septem Aeneas collectis navibus omni   170
ex numero subit ; ac magno telluris amore
egressi optata potiuntur Troes harena
et sale tabentes artus in litore ponunt.
ac primum silici scintillam excudit Achates
suscepitque ignem foliis atque arida circum   175
nutrimenta dedit rapuitque in fomite flammam.
tum Cererem corruptam undis Cerealiaque arma
expediunt fessi rerum, frugesque receptas
et torrere parant flammis et frangere saxo.
    Aeneas scopulum interea conscendit et omnem   180
prospectum late pelago petit, Anthea si quem
iactatum vento videat Phrygiasque biremes,
aut Capyn, aut celsis in puppibus arma Caici.
navem in conspectu nullam, tres litore cervos
prospicit errantes ; hos tota armenta sequuntur   185
a tergo, et longum per valles pascitur agmen.
constitit hic arcumque manu celeresque sagittas
corripuit, fidus quae tela gerebat Achates,
ductoresque ipsos primum capita alta ferentes
cornibus arboreis sternit ; tum vulgus et omnem   190
miscet agens telis nemora inter frondea turbam ;
nec prius absistit quam septem ingentia victor
corpora fundat humi et numerum cum navibus aequet.
hinc portum petit et socios partitur in omnes.
vina bonus quae deinde cadis onerarat Acestes   195

litore Trinacrio dederatque abeuntibus heros,
dividit, et dictis maerentia pectora mulcet :
' O socii (neque enim ignari sumus ante malorum),
o passi graviora, dabit deus his quoque finem.
vos et Scyllaeam rabiem penitusque sonantes   200
accestis scopulos, vos et Cyclopia saxa
experti : revocate animos, maestumque timorem
mittite ; forsan et haec olim meminisse iuvabit.
per varios casus, per tot discrimina rerum
tendimus in Latium, sedes ubi fata quietas   205
ostendunt ; illic fas regna resurgere Troiae.
durate, et vosmet rebus servate secundis.'
    Talia voce refert, curisque ingentibus aeger
spem vultu simulat, premit altum corde dolorem.
illi se praedae accingunt dapibusque futuris :   210
tergora diripiunt costis et viscera nudant ;
pars in frusta secant veribusque trementia figunt,
litore aëna locant alii flammasque ministrant.
tum victu revocant vires, fusique per herbam
implentur veteris Bacchi pinguisque ferinae.   215
postquam exempta fames epulis mensaeque remotae,
amissos longo socios sermone requirunt,
spemque metumque inter dubii, seu vivere credant
sive extrema pati nec iam exaudire vocatos.
praecipue pius Aeneas nunc acris Oronti,   220
nunc Amyci casum gemit et crudelia secum
fata Lyci fortemque Gyan fortemque Cloanthum.

Venus protests to Jupiter at the hard fate which dogs
Aeneas, her son.

Et iam finis erat, cum Iuppiter aethere summo
despiciens mare velivolum terrasque iacentes
litoraque et latos populos, sic vertice caeli   **225**
constitit et Libyae defixit lumina regnis.
atque illum tales iactantem pectore curas
tristior et lacrimis oculos suffusa nitentes
adloquitur Venus : ' o qui res hominumque deumque
aeternis regis imperiis et fulmine terres,   **230**
quid meus Aeneas in te committere tantum,
quid Troes potuere, quibus tot funera passis
cunctus ob Italiam terrarum clauditur orbis?
certe hinc Romanos olim volventibus annis,
hinc fore ductores, revocato a sanguine Teucri,   **235**
qui mare, qui terras omnes dicione tenerent,
pollicitus. quae te, genitor, sententia vertit?
hoc equidem occasum Troiae tristesque ruinas
solabar fatis contraria fata rependens ;
nunc eadem fortuna viros tot casibus actos   **240**
insequitur. quem das finem, rex magne, laborum?
Antenor potuit mediis elapsus Achivis
Illyricos penetrare sinus atque intima tutus
regna Liburnorum et fontem superare Timavi,
unde per ora novem vasto cum murmure montis   **245**
it mare proruptum et pelago premit arva sonanti.
hic tamen ille urbem Patavi sedesque locavit
Teucrorum, et genti nomen dedit armaque fixit
Troïa, nunc placida compostus pace quiescit :

nos, tua progenies, caeli quibus adnuis arcem,   250
navibus (infandum!) amissis, unius ob iram
prodimur atque Italis longe disiungimur oris.
hic pietatis honos? sic nos in sceptra reponis? '

*Jupiter reassures Venus with promises of the glorious destiny
in store for Aeneas and his Roman descendants, and
sends Mercury to ensure for Aeneas a welcome among the
Phoenicians.*

Olli subridens hominum sator atque deorum
vultu, quo caelum tempestatesque serenat,   255
oscula libavit natae, dehinc talia fatur :
' parce metu, Cytherea : manent immota tuorum
fata tibi ; cernes urbem et promissa Lavini
moenia, sublimemque feres ad sidera caeli
magnanimum Aenean ; neque me sententia vertit. 260
hic tibi (fabor enim, quando haec te cura remordet,
longius, et volvens fatorum arcana movebo)
bellum ingens geret Italia populosque feroces
contundet, moresque viris et moenia ponet,
tertia dum Latio regnantem viderit aestas,   265
ternaque transierint Rutulis hiberna subactis.
at puer Ascanius, cui nunc cognomen Iulo
additur (Ilus erat, dum res stetit Ilia regno),
triginta magnos volvendis mensibus orbes
imperio explebit, regnumque ab sede Lavini   270
transferet, et longam multa vi muniet Albam.
hic iam ter centum totos regnabitur annos
gente sub Hectorea, donec regina sacerdos

Marte gravis geminam partu dabit Ilia prolem.
inde lupae fulvo nutricis tegmine laetus　　　　　275
Romulus excipiet gentem, et Mavortia condet
moenia Romanosque suo de nomine dicet.
his ego nec metas rerum nec tempora pono :
imperium sine fine dedi.　quin aspera Iuno,
quae mare nunc terrasque metu caelumque fatigat, 280
consilia in melius referet, mecumque fovebit
Romanos, rerum dominos gentemque togatam.
sic placitum.　veniet lustris labentibus aetas,
cum domus Assaraci Phthiam clarasque Mycenas
servitio premet ac victis dominabitur Argis.　　　285
nascetur pulchra Troianus origine Caesar,
imperium Oceano, famam qui terminet astris,
Iulius, a magno demissum nomen Iulo.
hunc tu olim caelo, spoliis Orientis onustum,
accipies secura ; vocabitur hic quoque votis.　　290
aspera tum positis mitescent saecula bellis ;
cana Fides et Vesta, Remo cum fratre Quirinus
iura dabunt ; dirae ferro et compagibus artis
claudentur Belli portae ; Furor impius intus
saeva sedens super arma et centum vinctus aënis　295
post tergum nodis fremet horridus ore cruento.'
　　Haec ait, et Maia genitum demittit ab alto,
ut terrae utque novae pateant Karthaginis arces
hospitio Teucris, ne fati nescia Dido
finibus arceret.　volat ille per aëra magnum　　300
remigio alarum, ac Libyae citus astitit oris.
et iam iussa facit, ponuntque ferocia Poeni

corda volente deo ; in primis regina quietum
accipit in Teucros animum mentemque benignam.

*Aeneas, upon a journey of exploration, is met by Venus, dis-
guised as a huntress, who tells him of Dido, and her city of
Carthage now rising close at hand.*

At pius Aeneas, per noctem plurima volvens,   305
ut primum lux alma data est, exire locosque
explorare novos, quas vento accesserit oras,
qui teneant (nam inculta videt) hominesne feraene,
quaerere constituit sociisque exacta referre.
classem in convexo nemorum sub rupe cavata   310
arboribus clausam circum atque horrentibus umbris
occulit ; ipse uno graditur comitatus Achate,
bina manu lato crispans hastilia ferro.
cui mater media sese tulit obvia silva,
virginis os habitumque gerens et virginis arma,   315
Spartanae, vel qualis equos Threissa fatigat
Harpalyce volucremque fuga praevertitur Hebrum.
namque umeris de more habilem suspenderat arcum
venatrix, dederatque comam diffundere ventis,
nuda genu nodoque sinus collecta fluentes.   320
ac prior ' heus ' inquit, ' iuvenes, monstrate, mearum
vidistis si quam hic errantem forte sororum,
succinctam pharetra et maculosae tegmine lyncis,
aut spumantis apri cursum clamore prementem.'
    Sic Venus, et Veneris contra sic filius orsus :   325
'nulla tuarum audita mihi neque visa sororum,
o quam te memorem, virgo? namque haud tibi vultus

mortalis, nec vox hominem sonat ; o dea certe,
(an Phoebi soror an Nympharum sanguinis una?),
sis felix nostrumque leves, quaecumque, laborem,   330
et quo sub caelo tandem, quibus orbis in oris
iactemur doceas ; ignari hominumque locorumque
erramus, vento huc vastis et fluctibus acti :
multa tibi ante aras nostra cadet hostia dextra.'

Tum Venus : ' haud equidem tali me dignor honore;
virginibus Tyriis mos est gestare pharetram,   336
purpureoque alte suras vincire coturno.
Punica regna vides, Tyrios et Agenoris urbem ;
sed fines Libyci, genus intractabile bello.
imperium Dido Tyria regit urbe profecta,   340
germanum fugiens. longa est iniuria, longae
ambages ; sed summa sequar fastigia rerum.
huic coniunx Sychaeus erat, ditissimus agri
Phoenicum, et magno miserae dilectus amore,
cui pater intactam dederat primisque iugarat   345
ominibus. sed regna Tyri germanus habebat
Pygmalion, scelere ante alios immanior omnes.
quos inter medius venit furor. ille Sychaeum
impius ante aras atque auri caecus amore
clam ferro incautum superat, securus amorum   350
germanae ; factumque diu celavit, et aegram
multa malus simulans vana spe lusit amantem.
ipsa sed in somnis inhumati venit imago
coniugis, ora modis attollens pallida miris ;
crudeles aras traiectaque pectora ferro   355
nudavit, caecumque domus scelus omne retexit.

tum celerare fugam patriaque excedere suadet,
auxiliumque viae veteres tellure recludit
thesauros, ignotum argenti pondus et auri.
his commota fugam Dido sociosque parabat.   360
conveniunt quibus aut odium crudele tyranni
aut metus acer erat ; naves, quae forte paratae,
corripiunt onerantque auro.   portantur avari
Pygmalionis opes pelago ; dux femina facti.
devenere locos ubi nunc ingentia cernes   365
moenia surgentemque novae Karthaginis arcem,
mercatique solum, facti de nomine Byrsam,
taurino quantum possent circumdare tergo.
sed vos qui tandem, quibus aut venistis ab oris,
quove tenetis iter? ʼ quaerenti talibus ille   370
suspirans imoque trahens a pectore vocem :

*Venus bids Aeneas enter Dido's city of Carthage and tells him
    that his lost comrades shall be restored to him.   At parting
    she reveals herself for a moment in her divine form.*

ʻ O dea, si prima repetens ab origine pergam,
et vacet annales nostrorum audire laborum,
ante diem clauso componet Vesper Olympo.
nos Troia antiqua, si vestras forte per aures   375
Troiae nomen iit, diversa per aequora vectos
forte sua Libycis tempestas appulit oris.
sum pius Aeneas, raptos qui ex hoste penates
classe veho mecum, fama super aethera notus.
Italiam quaero patriam et genus ab Iove summo.   380
bis denis Phrygium conscendi navibus aequor,

matre dea monstrante viam, data fata secutus ;
vix septem convulsae undis Euroque supersunt.
ipse ignotus, egens, Libyae deserta peragro,
Europa atque Asia pulsus.' nec plura querentem   385
passa Venus medio sic interfata dolore est :
  ' Quisquis es, haud, credo, invisus caelestibus auras
vitales carpis, Tyriam qui adveneris urbem.
perge modo atque hinc te reginae ad limina perfer.
namque tibi reduces socios classemque relatam   390
nuntio et in tutum versis Aquilonibus actam,
ni frustra augurium vani docuere parentes.
aspice bis senos laetantes agmine cycnos,
aetheria quos lapsa plaga Iovis ales aperto
turbabat caelo ; nunc terras ordine longo   395
aut capere aut captas iam despectare videntur :
ut reduces illi ludunt stridentibus alis
et coetu cinxere polum cantusque dedere,
haud aliter puppesque tuae pubesque tuorum
aut portum tenet aut pleno subit ostia velo.   400
perge modo et, qua te ducit via, derige gressum.'
  Dixit, et avertens rosea cervice refulsit,
ambrosiaeque comae divinum vertice odorem
spiravere ; pedes vestis defluxit ad imos :
et vera incessu patuit dea. ille ubi matrem   405
agnovit tali fugientem est voce secutus :
' quid natum totiens, crudelis tu quoque, falsis
ludis imaginibus? cur dextrae iungere dextram
non datur ac veras audire et reddere voces? '
talibus incusat gressumque ad moenia tendit.   410

at Venus obscuro gradientes aëre saepsit,
et multo nebulae circum dea fudit amictu,
cernere ne quis eos neu quis contingere posset
molirive moram aut veniendi poscere causas.
ipsa Paphum sublimis abit sedesque revisit   415
laeta suas, ubi templum illi, centumque Sabaeo
ture calent arae sertisque recentibus halant.

*Aeneas and his companion Achates enter Carthage, where
building is in busy progress. They admire scenes from the
story of Troy, depicted in sculpture upon the buildings of the
city.*

Corripuere viam interea, qua semita monstrat.
iamque ascendebant collem, qui plurimus urbi
imminet adversasque aspectat desuper arces.   420
miratur molem Aeneas, magalia quondam,
miratur portas strepitumque et strata viarum.
instant ardentes Tyrii : pars ducere muros
molirique arcem et manibus subvolvere saxa,
pars optare locum tecto et concludere sulco.   425
iura magistratusque legunt sanctumque senatum.
hic portus alii effodiunt ; hic alta theatris
fundamenta locant alii, immanesque columnas
rupibus excidunt, scaenis decora alta futuris.
qualis apes aestate nova per florea rura   430
exercet sub sole labor, cum gentis adultos
educunt fetus, aut cum liquentia mella
stipant et dulci distendunt nectare cellas,
aut onera accipiunt venientum, aut agmine facto

DIDO AND AENEAS WITH VENUS AND CUPID DISGUISED AS ASCANIUS (See *Aeneid* I 657-756); panel from the Low Ham Villa mosaic).

ignavum fucos pecus a praesepibus arcent ;   **435**
fervet opus, redolentque thymo fragrantia mella.
' o fortunati, quorum iam moenia surgunt! '
Aeneas ait et fastigia suspicit urbis.
infert se saeptus nebula (mirabile dictu)
per medios miscetque viris, neque cernitur ulli.   **440**
    Lucus in urbe fuit media, laetissimus umbrae,
quo primum iactati undis et turbine Poeni
effodere loco signum, quod regia Iuno
monstrarat, caput acris equi : sic nam fore bello·
egregiam et facilem victu per saecula gentem.   **445**
hic templum Iunoni ingens Sidonia Dido

condebat, donis opulentum et numine divae,
aerea cui gradibus surgebant limina nexaeque
aere trabes, foribus cardo stridebat aënis.
hoc primum in luco nova res oblata timorem   450
leniit ; hic primum Aeneas sperare salutem
ausus et adflictis melius confidere rebus.
namque sub ingenti lustrat dum singula templo
reginam opperiens, dum quae fortuna sit urbi
artificumque manus intra se operumque laborem   455
miratur, videt Iliacas ex ordine pugnas
bellaque iam fama totum vulgata per orbem,
Atridas Priamumque et saevum ambobus Achillem.
constitit, et lacrimans ' quis iam locus,' inquit, ' Achate
quae regio in terris nostri non plena laboris?   460
en Priamus! sunt hic etiam sua praemia laudi ;
sunt lacrimae rerum et mentem mortalia tangunt.
solve metus ; feret haec aliquam tibi fama salutem.'
sic ait, atque animum pictura pascit inani
multa gemens, largoque umectat flumine vultum.   465
namque videbat uti bellantes Pergama circum
hac fugerent Grai, premeret Troiana iuventus,
hac Phryges, instaret curru cristatus Achilles.
nec procul hinc Rhesi niveis tentoria velis
agnoscit lacrimans, primo quae prodita somno   470
Tydides multa vastabat caede cruentus,
ardentesque avertit equos in castra, priusquam
pabula gustassent Troiae Xanthumque bibissent.
parte alia fugiens amissis Troilus armis,
infelix puer atque impar congressus Achilli,   475

fertur equis curruque haeret resupinus inani,
lora tenens tamen ; huic cervixque comaeque trahuntur
per terram, et versa pulvis inscribitur hasta.
interea ad templum non aequae Palladis ibant

ACHILLES SLAYS TROILUS.

crinibus Iliades passis peplumque ferebant,   480
suppliciter tristes et tunsae pectora palmis :
diva solo fixos oculos aversa tenebat.
ter circum Iliacos raptaverat Hectora muros
exanimumque auro corpus vendebat Achilles.
tum vero ingentem gemitum dat pectore ab imo,   485

AMAZONS AND GREEKS IN BATTLE.
(See note, l. 491).

ut spolia, ut currus, utque ipsum corpus amici
tendentemque manus Priamum conspexit inermes.
se quoque principibus permixtum agnovit Achivis,
Eoasque acies et nigri Memnonis arma.
ducit Amazonidum lunatis agmina peltis   490
Penthesilea furens mediisque in milibus ardet,
aurea subnectens exsertae cingula mammae,
bellatrix, audetque viris concurrere virgo.

Dido enters, and the companions of Aeneas, missing since the
tempest, appear and address to her an appeal for aid.

Haec dum Dardanio Aeneae miranda videntur,
dum stupet obtutuque haeret defixus in uno,   495
regina ad templum, forma pulcherrima Dido,
incessit magna iuvenum stipante caterva.
qualis in Eurotae ripis aut per iuga Cynthi
exercet Diana choros, quam mille secutae
hinc atque hinc glomerantur Oreades; illa pharetram 500
fert umero, gradiensque deas supereminet omnes;
(Latonae tacitum pertemptant gaudia pectus):
talis erat Dido, talem se laeta ferebat
per medios instans operi regnisque futuris.
tum foribus divae, media testudine templi,   505
saepta armis, solioque alte subnixa resedit.
iura dabat legesque viris, operumque laborem
partibus aequabat iustis aut sorte trahebat;
cum subito Aeneas concursu accedere magno
Anthea Sergestumque videt fortemque Cloanthum, 510
Teucrorumque alios, ater quos aequore turbo

dispulerat penitusque alias avexerat oras.
obstipuit simul ipse, simul percussus Achates
laetitiaque metuque : avidi coniungere dextras
ardebant, sed res animos incognita turbat.   515
dissimulant et nube cava speculantur amicti,

DEATH OF THE AMAZON PENTHESILEA.
Achilles supports the dying woman. The mourning
figure is another Amazon.

quae fortuna viris, classem quo litore linquant,
quid veniant : cunctis nam lecti navibus ibant
orantes veniam et templum clamore petebant.
    Postquam introgressi et coram data copia fandi,   520
maximus Ilioneus placido sic pectore coepit :
' o regina, novam cui condere Iuppiter urbem

iustitiaque dedit gentes frenare superbas,
Troes te miseri, ventis maria omnia vecti,
oramus : prohibe infandos a navibus ignes,   525
parce pio generi et propius res aspice nostras.
non nos aut ferro Libycos populare penates
venimus aut raptas ad litora vertere praedas ;
non ea vis animo nec tanta superbia victis.
est locus, Hesperiam Grai cognomine dicunt,   530
terra antiqua, potens armis atque ubere glaebae ;
Oenotri coluere viri ; nunc fama minores
Italiam dixisse ducis de nomine gentem ;
hic cursus fuit,
cum subito adsurgens fluctu nimbosus Orion   535
in vada caeca tulit, penitusque procacibus Austris
perque undas superante salo perque invia saxa
dispulit : huc pauci vestris adnavimus oris.
quod genus hoc hominum? quaeve hunc tam barbara
        morem
permittit patria? hospitio prohibemur harenae ;   540
bella cient primaque vetant consistere terra.
si genus humanum et mortalia temnitis arma,
at sperate deos memores fandi atque nefandi.
rex erat Aeneas nobis, quo iustior alter
nec pietate fuit, nec bello maior et armis :   545
quem si fata virum servant, si vescitur aura
aetheria neque adhuc crudelibus occubat umbris,
non metus, officio nec te certasse priorem
paeniteat : sunt et Siculis regionibus urbes
armaque, Troianoque a sanguine clarus Acestes.   550

quassatam ventis liceat subducere classem
et silvis aptare trabes et stringere remos,
si datur Italiam sociis et rege recepto
tendere, ut Italiam laeti Latiumque petamus ;
sin absumpta salus, et te, pater optime Teucrum,   555
pontus habet Libyae nec spes iam restat Iuli,
at freta Sicaniae saltem sedesque paratas,
unde huc advecti, regemque petamus Acesten.'
talibus Ilioneus ; cuncti simul ore fremebant
Dardanidae.   560

*Dido gives promise of assistance to the storm-tossed Trojans, and
Aeneas, till now, by the contrivance of Venus, invisible,
stands forth and thanks the queen for her humanity.*

Tum breviter Dido vultum demissa profatur :
' solvite corde metum, Teucri, secludite curas.
res dura et regni novitas me talia cogunt
moliri et late fines custode tueri.
quis genus Aeneadum, quis Troiae nesciat urbem,   565
virtutesque virosque aut tanti incendia belli?
non obtunsa adeo gestamus pectora Poeni,
nec tam aversus equos Tyria Sol iungit ab urbe.
seu vos Hesperiam magnam Saturniaque arva
sive Erycis fines regemque optatis Acesten,   570
auxilio tutos dimittam opibusque iuvabo.
vultis et his mecum pariter considere regnis?
urbem quam statuo, vestra est ; subducite naves ;
Tros Tyriusque mihi nullo discrimine agetur.
atque utinam rex ipse noto compulsus eodem   575

adforet Aeneas! equidem per litora certos
dimittam et Libyae lustrare extrema iubebo,
si quibus eiectus silvis aut urbibus errat.'
  His animum arrecti dictis et fortis Achates
et pater Aeneas iamdudum erumpere nubem   580
ardebant. prior Aenean compellat Achates :
' nate dea, quae nunc animo sententia surgit?
omnia tuta vides, classem sociosque receptos.
unus abest, medio in fluctu quem vidimus ipsi
summersum ; dictis respondent cetera matris.'   585
vix ea fatus erat cum circumfusa repente
scindit se nubes et in aethera purgat apertum.
restitit Aeneas claraque in luce refulsit
os umerosque deo similis ; namque ipsa decoram
caesariem nato genetrix lumenque iuventae   590
purpureum et laetos oculis adflarat honores :
quale manus addunt ebori decus, aut ubi flavo
argentum Pariusve lapis circumdatur auro.
tum sic reginam adloquitur cunctisque repente
improvisus ait : ' coram, quem quaeritis, adsum 595
Troius Aeneas, Libycis ereptus ab undis.
o sola infandos Troiae miserata labores,
quae nos, reliquias Danaum, terraeque marisque
omnibus exhaustis iam casibus, omnium egenos
urbe domo socias, grates persolvere dignas   600
non opis est nostrae, Dido, nec quidquid ubique est
gentis Dardaniae, magnum quae sparsa per orbem.
di tibi, si qua pios respectant numina, si quid
usquam iustitia est et mens sibi conscia recti,

praemia digna ferant. quae te tam laeta tulerunt 605
saecula? qui tanti talem genuere parentes?
in freta dum fluvii current, dum montibus umbrae
lustrabunt convexa, polus dum sidera pascet,
semper honos nomenque tuum laudesque manebunt,
quae me cumque vocant terrae.' sic fatus amicum 610
Ilionea petit dextra, laevaque Serestum,
post alios, fortemque Gyan fortemque Cloanthum.

*Dido makes Aeneas a speech of welcome. Sacrifices and a
banquet are ordered, and Achates is sent to fetch to the palace
Ascanius, the young son of Aeneas.*

Obstipuit primo aspectu Sidonia Dido,
casu deinde viri tanto, et sic ore locuta est :
'quis te, nate dea, per tanta pericula casus 615
insequitur? quae vis immanibus applicat oris?
tune ille Aeneas, quem Dardanio Anchisae
alma Venus Phrygii genuit Simoentis ad undam?
atque equidem Teucrum memini Sidona venire
finibus expulsum patriis, nova regna petentem 620
auxilio Beli ; genitor tum Belus opimam
vastabat Cyprum et victor dicione tenebat.
tempore iam ex illo casus mihi cognitus urbis
Troianae nomenque tuum regesque Pelasgi.
ipse hostis Teucros insigni laude ferebat, 625
seque ortum antiqua Teucrorum a stirpe volebat.
quare agite, o tectis, iuvenes, succedite nostris.
me quoque per multos similis fortuna labores
iactatam hac demum voluit consistere terra.

non ignara mali miseris succurrere disco.'   630
sic memorat ; simul Aenean in regia ducit
tecta, simul divum templis indicit honorem.
nec minus interea sociis ad litora mittit
viginti tauros, magnorum horrentia centum
terga suum, pingues centum cum matribus agnos,   635
munera laetitiamque dii.
at domus interior regali splendida luxu
instruitur, mediisque parant convivia tectis :
arte laboratae vestes ostroque superbo,
ingens argentum mensis, caelataque in auro   640
fortia facta patrum, series longissima rerum
per tot ducta viros antiqua ab origine gentis.
  Aeneas (neque enim patrius consistere mentem
passus amor) rapidum ad naves praemittit Achaten,
Ascanio ferat haec ipsumque ad moenia ducat ;   645
omnis in Ascanio cari stat cura parentis.
munera praeterea Iliacis erepta ruinis
ferre iubet, pallam signis auroque rigentem
et circumtextum croceo velamen acantho,
ornatus Argivae Helenae, quos illa Mycenis,   650
Pergama cum peteret inconcessosque hymenaeos,
extulerat, matris Ledae mirabile donum ;
praeterea sceptrum, Ilione quod gesserat olim,
maxima natarum Priami, colloque monile
bacatum, et duplicem gemmis auroque coronam.   655
haec celerans iter ad naves tendebat Achates.

Venus, for fear lest Dido should waver in her good will towards the exiles, substitutes for the boy Ascanius her own son, Cupid, meaning that he shall rouse in the queen a passion for Aeneas.

At Cythcrea novas artes, nova pectore versat
consilia, ut faciem mutatus et ora Cupido
pro dulci Ascanio veniat, donisque furentem
incendat rcginam atque ossibus implicet ignem.　660
quippe domum timet ambiguam Tyriosque bilingues,
urit atrox Iuno, et sub noctem cura recursat.
ergo his aligerum dictis adfatur Amorem :
' nate, meae vires, mea magna potentia, solus,
nate, patris summi qui tela Typhoëa temnis,　　665
ad tc confugio et supplex tua numina posco.
frater ut Aeneas pelago tuus omnia circum
litora iactetur odiis Iunonis acerbae,
nota tibi, et nostro doluisti saepe dolore.
nunc Phoenissa tenet Dido blandisque moratur　670
vocibus, et vereor quo se Iunonia vertant
hospitia ; haud tanto cessabit cardine rerum.
quocirca capere ante dolis et cingere flamma
reginam meditor, ne quo se numine mutet,
sed magno Aeneae mecum teneatur amore.　　675
qua facere id possis nostram nunc accipe mentem.
regius accitu cari genitoris ad urbem
Sidoniam puer ire parat, mea maxima cura,
dona terens pelago et flammis restantia Troiae ;
hunc ego sopitum somno super alta Cythera　680
aut super Idalium sacrata sede recondam,

ΖΕΥΣ

ZEUS (JUPITER) HURLS HIS THUNDERBOLT AT THE GIANT TYPHOEUS. .

ne qua scire dolos mediusve occurrere possit.
tu faciem illius noctem non amplius unam
falle dolo et notos pueri puer indue vultus,
ut, cum te gremio accipiet laetissima Dido

685

regales inter mensas laticemque Lyaeum,
cum dabit amplexus atque oscula dulcia figet,
occultum inspires ignem fallasque veneno.'
paret Amor dictis carae genetricis, et alas
exuit et gressu gaudens incedit Iuli.   690
at Venus Ascanio placidam per membra quietem
inrigat, et fotum gremio dea tollit in altos
Idaliae lucos, ubi mollis amaracus illum
floribus et dulci adspirans complectitur umbra.

*Cupid arrives in the likeness of Ascanius, and, fondled by Dido,
begins to awaken in her a love for Aeneas.*

Iamque ibat dicto parens et dona Cupido   695
regia portabat Tyriis duce laetus Achate.
cum venit, aulaeis iam se regina superbis
aurea composuit sponda mediamque locavit,
iam pater Aeneas et iam Troiana iuventus
conveniunt, stratoque super discumbitur ostro.   700
dant manibus famuli lymphas, Cereremque canistris
expediunt tonsisque ferunt mantelia villis.
quinquaginta intus famulae, quibus ordine longam
cura penum struere et flammis adolere penates ;
centum aliae totidemque pares aetate ministri,   705
qui dapibus mensas onerent et pocula ponant.
nec non et Tyrii per limina laeta frequentes
convenere, toris iussi discumbere pictis.
mirantur dona Aeneae, mirantur Iulum,
flagrantesque dei vultus simulataque verba   710
pallamque et pictum croceo velamen acantho.

praecipue infelix, pesti devota futurae,
expleri mentem nequit ardescitque tuendo
Phoenissa, et pariter puero donisque movetur.
ille ubi complexu Aeneae colloque pependit   715
et magnum falsi implevit genitoris amorem,
reginam petit. haec oculis, haec pectore toto
haeret et interdum gremio fovet inscia Dido
insidat quantus miserae deus. at memor ille
matris Acidaliae paulatim abolere Sychaeum   720
incipit et vivo temptat praevertere amore
iam pridem resides animos desuetaque corda.

*Dido and her guests drink together, and after listening to the
   minstrel Iopas, she invites Aeneas to tell the story of Troy's
   fall, and of his own subsequent wanderings.*

Postquam prima quies epulis mensaeque remotae,
crateras magnos statuunt et vina coronant.
fit strepitus tectis vocemque per ampla volutant   725
atria ; dependent lychni laquearibus aureis
incensi et noctem flammis funalia vincunt.
hic regina gravem gemmis auroque poposcit
implevitque mero pateram, quam Belus et omnes
a Belo soliti ; tum facta silentia tectis :   730
' Iuppiter, hospitibus nam te dare iura loquuntur,
hunc laetum Tyriisque diem Troiaque profectis
esse velis, nostrosque huius meminisse minores.
adsit laetitiae Bacchus dator et bona Iuno ;
et vos o coetum, Tyrii, celebrate faventes.'   735
dixit, et in mensam laticum libavit honorem

primaque, libato, summo tenus attigit ore ;
tum Bitiae dedit increpitans ; ille impiger hausit
spumantem pateram et pleno se proluit auro ;
post alii proceres. cithara crinitus Iopas   740
personat aurata, docuit quem maximus Atlas.
hic canit errantem lunam solisque labores,
unde hominum genus et pecudes, unde imber et ignes,
Arcturum pluviasque Hyadas geminosque Triones ;
quid tantum Oceano properent se tingere soles   745
hiberni, vel quae tardis mora noctibus obstet.
ingeminant plausu Tyrii, Troesque sequuntur.
nec non et vario noctem sermone trahebat
infelix Dido, longumque bibebat amorem,
multa super Priamo rogitans, super Hectore multa ; 750
nunc, quibus Aurorae venisset filius armis,
nunc, quales Diomedis equi, nunc, quantus Achilles.
' immo age, et a prima dic, hospes, origine nobis
insidias ' inquit ' Danaum casusque tuorum
erroresque tuos. nam te iam septima portat   755
omnibus errantem terris et fluctibus aestas.'

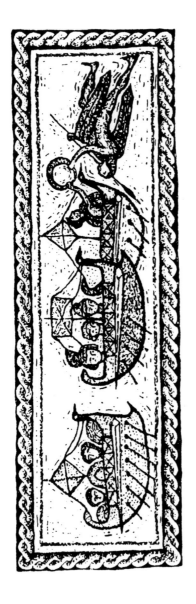

THE TROJAN FLEET: panel from the Low Ham Villa mosaic;
the panel probably shows the fleet arriving in Carthage with
Achates taking a gold collar for Dido. (See *Aeneid* I 645-655).

NOTES

Line 1. **Arma virumque.** From these famous opening words of Vergil's poem Shaw took the title of his comedy, ' Arms and the Man '. **Arma,** ' weapons ', is put poetically for ' war '

virum. ' The man ' is the hero of the epic, the Trojan prince Aeneas.

cano. It is now a mere convention that poets ' sing '. But the poetry of ancient Greece and Rome, written for recitation rather than reading, was often declaimed against a background of instrumental music, and what we call ' lyric ' poetry was actually sung.

Troiae. The ancient city of Troy was situated near the Asiatic entrance to the Dardanelles. Its siege and capture by the Greeks made one of the greatest stories of antiquity. **Troiae,** gen., depends on **oris.**

ll. 2, 3. **Italiam Lavinaque litora,** ' to Italy ', etc. In Latin poetry the accusative without **ad** is occasionally used to express the goal of motion.

l. 2. **fato** is to be taken closely with **profugus.**

l. 3. **multum,** adverb, goes with **iactatus. ille,** not required grammatically, helps to remind us, after a line and a half, that the subject is ' the man ' : ' much harassed . . . he '.

et terris et alto, ' both on land and on the deep '. Two things common in Latin poetry are to be noticed here : first, the use of the plural **terris** for the singular **terra**—this looseness in regard to number occurs very frequently, while, conversely, the singular is often put for the plural ; and second, the absence of the preposition **in,** a very common omission.

l. 4. **vi.** The ablative goes with **iactatus** : ' harassed by . . .'

superum, gen. pl. For this case of the second declension the **-um** form is older than **-orum**. You will meet later, l. 9, **deum** for **deorum**.

memorem, from the adjective **memor**. The word qualifies **iram,** which is governed by **ob**.

saevae Iunonis. Juno, wife of Jupiter and chief among the goddesses, was the bitter enemy of the Trojans, and so of Aeneas, because the Trojan Paris had judged her to be inferior in beauty to Venus.

l. 5. The **et** is misplaced and should be taken as the first word in the line.

multa, acc. pl. neut., 'many things', 'much', object of **passus**.

quŏque, 'also'. Do not confuse this with **quōque**, from **quisque,** 'each'.

bello, '*in* war'.

passus, participle from the deponent verb **patior**. It may be rendered 'suffering', as perfect participles of deponent verbs may have a present meaning.

dum conderet. **dum,** 'until', is used here with the subjunctive because Aeneas' *willingness* to suffer *in order to found* his new city is implied, and makes the **dum conderet** not merely a time clause, but a final clause as well. The same applies to **inferret**.

l. 6. **deos.** Aeneas had rescued from burning Troy certain images of the Trojan gods, and proposes to introduce their worship into Italy.

Latio, dative, 'into Latium'. This is another poetical construction, and a prose writer would have put **in Latium**. Latium was a small district of Italy in the angle formed by the Tiber and the west coast to the southward of it. It was the cradle of Roman power.

genus unde Latinum. **unde,** normally 'whence' = 'from whom' here. **genus, patres** and **moenia** are all nominative case, subjects to some such verb understood as 'proceeded'. 'sprang'.

l. 7. **Albani patres,** ' the Alban fathers '. There is probably
a reference in the word **patres** to the fact that many patrician
families claimed to have originated in Alba Longa, a city
which according to tradition was founded by Aeneas' son,
Iulus. Among these families were the Iulii, who claimed
descent from Iulus, and it must be remembered that Virgil
had a political purpose in writing the Aeneid at the suggestion
of Augustus, namely to surround what was virtually a usurpa-
tion by the Julian house with an aura of antiquity and divine
sanction.

Romae. Rome comes last in this catalogue because it was
founded later than Alba Longa, by Romulus, a descendant of
Aeneas.

l. 8. **Musa,** vocative. It was customary for a poet to invoke
the aid of one of the Muses at the commencement of a long
poem. The Muses, nine in number, were goddesses worshipped
as the patrons of literature and the arts. The Muse of epic
poetry was called Calliope.

ll. 8-11. The general idea is : Tell me, Muse, what made
Juno so angry as to persecute Aeneas, a thoroughly good man.
Can gods feel such resentment?

l. 8. **memora,** imperative. The verb **memoro** means
' recount ', not ' remember '.

quo numine laeso, ' because of what injured majesty ', i.e.
' for what affront to her majesty '. This ablative, expressing
' because of ', is the ablative of cause.

l. 9. **quidve dolens,** ' or resenting what ', i.e. ' or by what
enraged '. Notice the particle **-ve,** ' or ', attached (like **-que,**
' and ') to the end of the word before which it must be taken.

ll. 9-11. **regina deum . . . impulerit,** ' did the queen of the
gods force a man remarkable for his righteousness to pass
through (**volvere**) so many perils, to encounter so many
tribulations.'

l. 9. **regina deum** is Juno. **deum** gen. pl. ; cf. **superum,** l. 4.

volvere, literally ' roll ', is put poetically for ' pass through '.

One of the features that distinguishes poetry from prose is its avoidance of the obvious word.

volvere, adire. These infinitives would in prose be **ut** clauses with the subjunctive.

casūs, acc. pl., object of **volvere.**

l. 10. **pietate.** pietas means ' dutifulness ', whether of the creature to his god, of the son to his parents, of the citizen to his state. pius is the adjective regularly applied by Vergil to Aeneas, who shows this quality in all the three forms mentioned above.

labores. Notice this secondary meaning of the word, ' trouble '.

l. 11. **impulerit,** subjunctive in the indirect question introduced by the interrogatives **quo** and **quid.**

tantaene, etc. ' (Are there) to divine hearts such great angers? ' i.e. ' Do breasts divine harbour such deep resentment? ' For the pl. irae see note on **terris,** l. 3.

ll. 12-33. In these lines the poet gives another reason for Juno's hostility to Aeneas : she is the patroness of Carthage, and has learned that it is fated to be destroyed by descendants of Aeneas.

l. 12. **Tyrii tenuere coloni.** ' Tyrian settlers ', because Carthage was a colony of the Phoenicians, one of whose chief cities Tyre was. **tenuere,** alternative form for **tenuerunt.**

l. 13. **contra,** ' opposite ', ' facing ', governs **Italiam** and **ostia.**

l. 14. Carthage, near the modern Tunis, lies across the Mediterranean from Rome.

l. 14. **dives** and **asperrima** are in apposition to **urbs,** l. 12.

opum, ' in resources '. The genitive is similar to those which more naturally follow words like **plenus,** ' full '.

studiisque asperrima belli, ' and very formidable in the practice of war '. **asper** is literally ' rough ', and **studiis,** abl. of respect, indicates the sphere in which the city's roughness is shown, or was developed.

l. 15. **quam.** It is unnatural in English to use the relative pronoun after a major stop. For **quam unam** say, ' this one city '. It is the object of **coluisse.**

fertur, ' is said ', a not uncommon meaning of **fero** in poetry. Take **coluisse** immediately after **Iuno fertur.**

terris omnibus, the ablative of comparison, expressing ' than ' after the comparative adverb **magis.**

l. 16. **posthabita Samo,** the ablative absolute, or ablative of attendant circumstances, ' Samos having been put second '. We may say ' esteeming (even) Samos less '. **posthabitā,** because **Samos** is a feminine noun.

Juno might have been expected to hold Samos (an island off the coast of Asia Minor) particularly dear, because it was her birthplace, and a centre of her worship.

arma, supply **fuerunt. hic** is the adverb.

ll. 17, 18. The order for translation is, **iam tum dea tenditque fovetque hoc esse gentibus regnum, si quā fata sinant. iam tum** we take in reverse order, ' then already ', i.e. even in those early days of history.

tendit and **fovet** are historic presents, and the first -que = ' both ', and may be dropped. Translate : ' even then the goddess aimed and desired that this (i.e. Carthage) should be for the nations the-seat-of-sovereignty (**regnum**), if the fates should in-any-way (**quā**) allow it '.

hoc esse. The accusative and infinitive is not really appropriate in dependence upon the verbs **tendit** and **fovet**, but would suit **vult** well enough, to which these two verbs are here virtually equivalent.

sinant. The subjunctive seems to mark that the clause represents a quotation from Juno's thoughts—**fata sinant,** ' may the fates allow it '. Notice the suggestion that the fates are the ultimate powers, and above even the gods.

l. 19. **sed enim.** When these words occur together **enim** means ' indeed ' or ' in truth '.

dūci—distinguish **dŭci,** from **dux**—is present infinitive passive, and **progeniem duci** is acc. and infin. dependent on **audierat** : ' she had heard that a breed was rising ' (lit. ' being drawn ').

l. 20. The order is **quae verteret olim Tyrias arces. quae verteret** is final and means ' to overthrow '. Final (purpose) clauses are often introduced by the relative pronoun instead of by **ut.**

Tyrias arces, i.e. Carthage, ' Tyrian ' because Dido its foundress came from Tyre.

ll. 20, 21 are still in the accusative and infinitive, dependent on **audierat.**

l. 21. **hinc,** ' from this (breed) '.

late regem, ' widely king ', i.e. ' holding wide power '.

bello, ' in war ', with **superbum.**

l. 22. **venturum,** i.e. **venturum esse,** ' should come '.

excidio, dative of purpose, ' for the destruction '.

Libyae, put poetically for **Carthaginis.**

sic volvere Parcas, ' that in this way the Fates were tending '. **volvere,** which usually means ' roll ' (transitive), is used here intransitively.

l. 23. **Saturnia,** ' daughter of Saturn ', i.e. Juno.

belli is the *objective* genitive. It will be seen that **belli** bears the same relation to **memor** as does **id,** the accusative object, to **metuens.**

l. 24. **quod,** relative pronoun, is to be taken first in this line.

prima, in grammar an adjective, qualifying the understood subject of **gesserat,** has the force of an adverb, ' before '.

ad Troiam. ad here has the meaning ' at '. The locative **Troiae** would mean ' in ', while **ad Troiam** suggests the situation of a besieging force outside the city.

pro caris Argis. Just as **Libyae,** l. 22, was put for the more circumscribed **Carthaginis,** so, conversely, Vergil uses the name of the town **Argos** instead of that of the country, **Graecia.**

Juno's favour was not in reality limited to the single Greek city of Argos but extended to the Greeks generally.

l. 25. **necdum etiam,** ' and not even yet '.

causae and **dolores** appear more natural as singulars in English.

l. 26. **alta mente,** ' in her deep mind ', but the English idiom is ' deep in her mind '. Notice the absence of the preposition **in.**

manet, though singular, has four subjects, **iudicium, iniuria, genus, honores,** and agrees with the first of them only.

l. 27. **iudicium Paridis.** ' The judgment of Paris ' refers to the myth that Paris, a Trojan prince, was called in to award a golden apple to the most beautiful of the goddesses, an honour claimed by Juno, Venus and Minerva. All three competitors attempted to bribe the judge, and Paris gave the prize to Venus, who had promised him the lovely Helen. This judgment was the prime cause of Juno's resentment against the Trojans.

spretae iniuria formae, ' the insult of (i.e. consisting in) her beauty scorned '. This is again a reference to the judgment of Paris. The fact that in Latin all relations between nouns are expressed by the genitive case leads to the occurrence of many genitives which seem remote in meaning from the standard ' of '. **Ganymedis** in the next line is another example of a difficult genitive.

l. 28. **genus invisum,** ' the hateful race '. We should say rather, ' her hatred for the (Trojan) race '. This may allude to an earlier cause of the ill will felt by Juno for the Trojans— the fact that they sprang from a mortal woman, Electra, who was loved by Juno's consort, Jupiter.

rapti Ganymedis honores, ' the honours *paid to* the ravished Ganymede '. Notice how the genitive **Ganymedis** has to be translated here, the difficulty arising from the fact that if one noun is to be made dependent on another it must be put in the genitive case.

Ganymedis. Ganymede was a beautiful boy who became the

favourite of Jupiter and thus aroused Juno's jealousy. The fact that he, like Paris, was a Trojan, added fuel to Juno's anger against that race.

l. 29. **accensa**, which agrees with **Saturnia**, l. 23, resumes the construction of the interrupted sentence : 'inflamed further (**super**) by these things, she . . .'

iactatos, ' (tempest)-tossed ', agrees with **Troas**, l. 30, which is acc. pl. masc. according to a Greek form, and the object of **arcebat**.

aequore toto, ' in every (quarter of) the sea '. Even in prose, ' place ' phrases that include the word **totus** are commonly used without the preposition **in**.

l. 30. **reliquias** is in apposition to **Troas**. **Danaum** and **Achilli** are further instances of awkward genitives : ' the remnant *left by* the Greeks and ruthless Achilles ', i.e. the survivors from the sack of Troy.

l. 31. **Latio**, ' from Latium ', depends on **longe**.

l. 32. **maria omnia**, acc. governed by the preposition **circum**.

l. 33. **tantae molis erat**, lit. ' of such great effort it was ', i.e. ' so hard a task it was.' To English minds there appears to be missing some such word as **opus**, ' task ', for **tantae molis** to depend on, but the omission is regular in Latin.

l. 34. **in altum**, ' into the deep ', i.e. ' for the open sea '.

l. 35. **laeti**, ' joyously '. Adjectives are often used in Latin where English prefers adverbs.

aere, ' with bronze ', i.e., ' with bronze-sheathed prow '. Ancient men-of-war had sharp metal rams.

l. 36. **servans**, ' keeping ', but our idiom is ' nursing '.

sub, usually ' under ', sometimes has the force of ' deep in '.

vulnus. This ' wound ' is the insult offered her by Paris, coupled with the grievance mentioned in l. 28, and what Juno ' nurses ' is really the sense of outrage thereby provoked.

l. 37. **haec** is the object of a verb to be supplied, say **locuta est**. Note that this missing verb would be indicative, as the conjunction **cum** introduces what is virtually, though not grammatically, the principal clause of the sentence. Such clauses are called ' inverse **cum** ' clauses, and the indicative is regular in them.

secum. English says ' *to* herself '.

The order for the next four words is **mene victam desistere incepto,** and the construction is the accusative and infinitive used independently as an exclamation : ' What! I, defeated, cease from my endeavour . . .' **mene** is the accusative of **ego** plus the interrogative particle -ne, and **incepto** is ablative.

l. 38. **Italia. Ab Italia** in prose.

regem, i.e., Aeneas.

l. 39. **quippe vetor fatis.** This is ironical, for Juno's real meaning, ' the fates do not forbid me ', is the opposite of what she actually says. Translate : ' the Fates, I suppose, forbid me.'

ll. 39-45. General sense : the goddess Athena destroyed a whole fleet for one man's sin (so I claim the same right).

l. 40. **ipsos,** ' (the men) themselves '.

ponto, ' *in* the sea ', the ' local ' ablative without preposition.

l. 41. **unius.** The ' one man ' is Ajax.

Oilei, ' (son) of Oileus '. This omission of such words as ' son ', ' daughter ' is common. The word is here scanned Oīleī, the final **ei** being run together into a single sound, approximately **yi.**

furias. His ' madness ' consisted in his defiance of the gods.

Aiacis. Two Greek heroes of the Trojan war bore the name Ajax. The one here mentioned is the less famous. His offence against Athena was an act of sacrilege committed in her temple.

l. 42. **ipsa,** ' herself ', i.e. Pallas. Say, ' with her own hand '.

iaculata, i.e. **iaculata est.** This omission of the auxiliary from passive and deponent forms is not uncommon.

ignem Iovis, i.e. the lightning.

I. 44. The object of the sentence comes first : ' him, breathing forth flames from his pierced breast, she . . .' The lightning stroke had carried fire into the body of Ajax, and his breath as he exhaled was fiery.

l. 45. **scopulo**, ' upon a rock '.

l. 46. **divum.** For the gen. pl. cf. note on **superum**, l. 4.

incedo, 'move in majesty '. The word is mostly used of solemn progress such as that of gods.

regina is nominative in opposition to **quae.**

ll. 46, 47. -**que** . . . **et** . . . **et**, ' and both . . . and . . .'

l. 47. **et soror et coniunx.** Juno and Jupiter were both children of Saturn.

una cum gente, i.e. the Trojans.

l. 48. **gero.** The present is used because she is still at war. English in such cases prefers the perfect.

bella is a poetic plural, and should be rendered by the singular.

l. 49. **supplex**, ' humbly '. See note on **laeti**, l. 35.

aris, ' upon her altars '. The case is probably dative. Many verbs compounded with prepositions take this case.

l. 50. **Talia**, ' such (thoughts), acc., object of **volutans** '.

secum, ' with herself ', i.e. ' inwardly '.

ll. 51, 52. The order for translation is **venit in Aeoliam, patriam nimborum, loca feta furentibus Austris.**

l. 51. **loca**. **Locus** has two plurals, **loci** = ' (particular) places ' and **loca** = ' a region '.

l. 52. **hic**, adverb, ' here '.

vasto antro, ' local ' ablative without preposition.

l. 54. **vinclis et carcere**, lit. ' with chains and a prison ', a way of saying ' with imprisoning chains '. This idiom, by which a noun ' prison ' is put instead of an adjective, ' imprisoning ', is called hendiadys. Compare **pateris libamus et**

auro, 'we pour a drink offering from golden bowls' (lit. 'bowls and gold ').

l. 55. **magno cum murmure montis,** lit., 'with great murmur of the mountain ', i.e. ' while the mountain moans loudly '. The **murmur** is produced by the winds' struggles to escape from their prison inside the mountain.

l. 56. **celsa arce,** local ablative without preposition.

l. 57. **sceptra,** pl. put for sing. as often in Latin poetry.

animos, iras, i.e. of the winds.

l. 58. **ni** = **nisi.**

ll. 58, 59. **faciat, ferant, verrant.** The present subjunctive in conditional sentences relates to future time. Thus **ni faciat, ferant** = ' if he were not to do (so), they would carry away . . .' **ferant** here = **auferant.**

l. 58. **profundum.** We should say ' high ' rather than ' deep '. The use of the single Latin word **altus** for both these notions underlines their essential sameness.

l. 59. **rapidi,** adjective for adverb again, as so often.

verrant. The object is ' them ' understood, i.e. sea, earth and heaven.

l. 60. **pater omnipotens,** i.e. Jupiter.

speluncis, local ablative without preposition.

l. 61. **molem et montes altos.** For **molem et montes** cf. **vinclis et carcere,** l. 54, and the note on those words. This is hendiadys again : the noun **molem,** ' mass ' is put instead of ' massive ', qualifying **montes.** The whole expression = ' high and massive mountains '.

ll. 62, 63. **qui sciret,** ' who should know '. The subjunctive is ' generic '. When the relative pronoun approximates in meaning to ' the kind of person who ' it is regularly followed by the subjunctive mood. Remember that **genus,** from which ' generic ' is derived, means ' kind '. Compare **ea est Romana gens quae victa quiescere nesciat,** ' the Roman race is one that

(=of such a kind that), when vanquished, knows not how to rest quiet.'

l. 62. **foedere certo,** ' under a fixed covenant '. The appointed king of the winds contracted with Jupiter, as it were, to keep them under control.

l. 63. The first **et** =' both '.

premere, ' (how) to tighten '.

laxas dare, lit. ' to give loose ', forms one notion, ' to slacken '.

iussus, ' (as) ordered ', i.e. by Jupiter.

habenas, ' reins ', connected with **habeo,** ' hold '. The use of this word, by which the winds are compared to a team of horses, constitutes a metaphor.

l. 64. **ad quem.** The use of the relative pronoun after a major stop is unnatural in English. We should say ' to him ' rather than ' to whom '.

supplex, adj. for adv. Cf. l. 35.

vocibus, abl., governed by **usa est. vox** here, as not infrequently in poetry, means ' word '.

l. 65. **namque.** The clause introduced by this word modifies one that is not expressed, but is left to be understood from the vocative **Aeole** : ' Aeolus (to thee I speak), for to thee . . . the father . . . gave '.

divum. See note on **superum,** l. 4.

l. 66. **mulcere** and **tollere** are objects of **dedit.** In English we should say ' gave (power) to calm ', etc.

l. 67. **mihi** goes closely with **inimica.**

Tyrrhenum aequor. This is the sea to the westward of the Italian peninsula, and is so called because it washes the shores of Tyrrhenia, ' Etruria ' or ' Tuscany '.

l. 68. **Ilium** is another name for Troy. The fleet may be said to ' carry Ilium to Italy ' in the sense that Aeneas is preparing to introduce Trojan customs and worship there.

l. 69. **incute vim ventis,** lit. ' strike violence into thy winds '.

The sense must be ' infuriate the winds by striking them', which can best be conveyed by ' goad thy winds to fury '. **ventis** is a dative similar to **aris**, l. 49.

summersas obrue puppes, lit. ' overwhelm the sunken ships ', is quite natural Latin for ' sink and overwhelm the ships '. In fact, when a subject has two verbs, it is perhaps more usual to express the first of the two actions, as here, by a perfect participle passive in agreement with the direct object.   Cf. **nuntium captum interfecerunt,** normal Latin for ' they caught and killed the messenger '.

l. 70. **age diversos** is a single notion expressed by two words, rather like **laxas dare,** l. 63.   ' Drive different ways ' = ' scatter '. Notice that **diversos,** masc. pl., agrees with the understood object, **homines,** of **age.**

ponto, ' on the sea ', the local ablative without preposition again.

ll. 71-75. Juno seeks to bribe Aeolus to do her will.

l. 71. **sunt mihi,** ' there are to me ' is a common way of saying ' I have '.   In this idiom **mihi** is called the dative of the possessor.   Naturally, the subject of **sunt, Nymphae,** becomes in translation the object of ' I have '.

bis septem, poetic for **quattuordecim.**

praestanti corpore is the ablative of description, which always consists of two words, noun and adjective, and is equivalent to an English phrase with ' of '.   **corpore** here = **forma,** and we may say ' of surpassing beauty '.

ll. 72, 73. ' of whom I will join (to thee) in abiding wedlock (her) who (is) fairest of form, Deiopea, and will make (her) thine own.'

forma is ablative of respect, modifying **pulcherrima.**   Cf. **pauci numero,** ' few in number '.

Deiopea, five syllables.

conubio stabili, ablative of manner indicating the *way* in which Juno will join the nymph to Aeolus.   This ablative, like the ablative of description above, l. 71, normally consists of two words.

l. 74. **omnes,** acc. pl. masc.

meritis pro talibus, i.e. in return for Aeolus' being willing to gratify Juno in the matter of the destruction of the Trojan fleet.

l. 75. **exigat, faciat,** subjunctives in final (purpose) clauses, following upon **ut** meaning ' in order that '.

pulchra prole. Proceed as if this were a genitive dependent on **parentem.**

l. 76. **haec** is object of some such verb as **dixit,** to be supplied, and **contra** an adv. ' in reply '.

ll. 76, 77. **tuus,** etc. ' (It is) thy task to search out what thou desirest,' i.e. the only labour required of the august queen of heaven is the formulation of her own desires. **optes** is subjunctive in an indirect question, i.e. a noun clause introduced by an interrogative word.

l. 77. **iussa,** supply **tua.**

ll. 78-80. Aeolus gives other reasons for acceding to Juno's request. He owes her everything, he says. Note the repetition of **tu,** and its emphatic position.

l. 78. **quodcumque hoc regni,** ' whatever this (is) of sovereignty ', i.e. ' this sovereignty, such as it is '. The King of the Winds speaks deprecatingly of his own station, not contemptuously—which would be tactless—of Juno's gift. The expression **quodcumque hoc regni** is object of **concilias,** as are **sceptra** and **Iovem. sceptra** is pl. for sg., and **Iovem** must be translated ' (the favour) of Jove '. **Concilio** really means ' win over ', but this would only be a suitable translation with **Iovem.**

l. 79. **epulis,** ' at the banquets ', probably dative after the compound verb **accumbere.**

accumbere, ' (the right) to take my place '. For the infinitive as direct object of **dare,** cf. l. 63, where it was necessary to translate **premere** ' (power) to tighten '. **accumbere** means properly ' to recline ', the usual posture of Roman diners.

divum, gen. pl.

l. 80. **potentem**, lit., 'powerful', but translate by a noun ' lord '. It agrees with **me** understood, object of **facis**.

l. 81. **haec ubi dicta**, i.e. **ubi haec dicta (sunt)**.

conversa cuspide. ablative absolute, ' his spear having been reversed ', i.e. ' reversing his spear '. Aeolus used the butt, not the point.

ll. 81, 82. **cavum montem in latus**, ' the hollow mountain against its side ', a way of saying ' the side of the hollow mountain '. Aeolus breached the wall of the cave to allow the winds to escape.

l. 82. **velut agmine facto**, abl. abs., lit., ' as if a column having been made ', i.e. ' like an ordered host '.

l. 83. **qua** is an adverb, ' where '.

data (est) porta, ' a gate has been given (them) '.

terras, ' lands ', i.e. ' the world '.

perflant, like **ruunt**, is a historic present. In the following three lines, which contain three verbs, a perfect is followed by two more historic presents.

l. 84. **mari**, dative after compound verb **incubuere** (=incubuerunt). This verb has three subjects, all names of winds, Eurus, the East Wind, Notus the South Wind, and Africus, the wind from Africa, i.e. the South Wester. With this last goes the adjectival phrase **creber procellis**, ' frequent with squalls ', or as we should say ' with its frequent squalls '.

totum, acc. sg. neut., agrees with **id** (=mare) understood, and is the object of **ruunt** in a different sense from that employed in l. 83 : ' heave (it) all up '.

l. 85. **una**, an adverb, ' together '.

l. 87. **clamorque**. The **-que** = ' both '. Similarly **caelumque**, l. 88.

virum, gen. pl. ' The men ' are the sailors of the Trojan fleet.

stridorque rudentum. The rigging of the ships groans under the strain imposed by the gale.

diem, ' the daylight '.

l. 89. **ponto,** dative after the compound verb **incubat.**

l. 90. **intonuere,** being coupled, like **incubuere,** l. 84, with historic presents, may itself be more naturally translated by the present tense.

l. 91. **omnia** is nom.

Notice the construction with the verb **intentant**—acc. of thing threatened, dat. of person. In English we threaten a person *with* a thing.

l. 92. **solvuntur** suggests the paralysing weakness induced by terror.

frigore. The word usually means ' cold '. Here it is plainly ' cold fear '.

l. 93. **tendens palmas.** The ancients prayed not as we do, but with the hands held up before the face, wrists bent and palms uppermost and horizontal.

l. 94. **beati,** vocative.

l. 95. **quīs** is another form of **quibus,** dat. pl. masc., and depends on **contigit** : ' (you) to whom it befell . . .' **contingo** is used of fortunate happenings, and the misery of Aeneas is such that he is envious of those Trojans who perished in the war.

ora, from **ōs.**

Danaum, gen. pl., dependent on **gentis.**

l. 96. **fortissimĕ,** voc. with **Tydide.** Contrast **fortissimē,** superl. adv.

l. 97. **Tydide.** The ending **-ides** in Greek names represents ' son of '. The ' son of Tydeus ' was Diomedes, a warrior who fought with Aeneas in the war, and by whom he says he wishes he had been killed.

ll. 97, 98. **mene occumbere non potuisse.** The construction is the same as that in ll. 37, 38 : ' (to think) that I could not fall . . .'

l. 97. **Iliacis campis.** You should now be familiar with this ablative of place without the preposition **in,** and it will not in future always be noted.

l. 98. **tuaque,** etc., lit. ' and pour out this life by thy right hand '. Say ' and spill my life's blood, (slain) by thy hand '.

l. 99. **Aeacidae.** The ' son of Aeacus ' is Achilles, greatest warrior among the Greeks. For the **-ides** termination cf. **Tydide,** l. 97.

telo, abl. of the instrument with **iacet,** which = ' lies dead '. The second **ubi** understands **iacet** repeated.

l. 100. **Sarpedon,** an ally of the Trojans, killed by Patroclus, the friend of Achilles.

Simois (three syllables), a river near Troy.

ll. 100, 101. **correpta volvit.** This is the same construction as that noted on l. 69—**summersas obrue puppes**—and must be dealt with in the same way, i.e. proceed as if you had **corripit et volvit.**

tot and **fortia** belong in grammar with **scuta** and **corpora** respectively, but in sense with **virum** (gen. pl.), which is dependent on all three words—**scuta, galeas, corpora.** Say ' the shields, the helmets and the bodies of so many gallant men '. **tot** and **fortia** are called ' transferred epithets ' and the practice of so using adjectives is called *hypallage.* Cf. **Tyrrhenus tubae clangor,** for ' the blare of a Tuscan trumpet ', and in English, ' the ploughman homeward plods his weary way '.

ll. 102, 103. The literal translation is : ' (for him) hurling such (cries) a squall, shrieking with the North Wind, strikes (his) sail square(ly) '. **iactanti** agrees with **ei** understood, a dative of the person interested—the sufferer by the gust is Aeneas. Begin : ' as he utters such cries . . .'

l. 103. **adversa.** The Trojan fleet is in the Tyrrhene sea (l. 67), bound for Italy (l. 68), i.e. steering approximately north. The blast from the north therefore strikes the sail from ahead, and this is what **adversa** means.

l. 104. **franguntur remi.** The ship is under both oar and sail, and the violent gust from ahead puts too much strain on the oars, which are moving the ship in the contrary direction, and they snap.

prora avertit. The verb is here used intransitively : 'the stem swings off '.

l. 105. **dat,** ' presents ' or ' exposes '.

cumulo belongs in grammar with **praeruptus,** lit. ' precipitous in a heap '. **praeruptus** indicates that the mountain of water is vertical, **cumulo** adds the notions of height and weight : say, ' there ensues a sheer, towering mountain of water '.

l. 106. **hi, his**—the sailors of the fleet, equivalent to **alii aliis,** ' some (of the sailors) . . . , to others . . .'

unda, ' sea '.

l. 107. **terram,** i.e. the sea-bed.

aperit, ' reveals '.

aestus, usually ' tide ', here used generally for ' water '.

furit harenis. The very sand of the sea-bed is stirred by the tempest's violence and clouds the water with its agitated particles.

l. 108. **tres,** acc. pl. fem., agrees with **naves** understood. **abreptas torquet = abripit et torquet.** Cf. **summersas obrue** and the note, l. 69, also **correpta volvit,** ll. 100, 101. **abreptas,** like **tres,** goes with **naves** understood.

l. 109. Begin with **saxa quae,** ' rocks which '.

mediis. medius, an adjective, answers to the English ' in the midst of ' just as **summus,** l. 110 = ' the surface of '.

l. 110. **dorsum immane** is acc., in apposition to **saxa,** l. 109, which in turn is in apposition to the first **saxa,** l. 108.

mari summo. Here ' the Altars ' are described as being

' on the surface of the sea ', in l. 108 they are called ' hidden '. But there is no inconsistency. The broken water may be supposed to obscure what is normally visible.

ab alto, ' from deep water '.

miserabile visu, ' a piteous sight '. But the grammar is ' piteous in the seeing ', **visu** being an abl. (of respect) from the verbal noun derived from **video.** This noun occurs usually in two cases only, acc. and abl., and these forms are often called the *supine* in -**um** and the *supine* in -**u** respectively. The only use of the latter is, as in the present case, to limit the meaning of an adjective. Cf. **mirabile dictu,** ' marvellous to relate '.

l. 112. **inlidit.** Supply **eas** (= **naves**) as object, and again as object of **cingit. vadis,** ' upon shoals ', is the dative so often found in association with verbs compounded with prepositions.

aggere cingit harenae. The second three ships become partially engulfed in the sand-banks upon which they are driven.

l. 113. **unam,** supply **navem.**

Lycios. The Lycians had been allies of the Trojans in the late war.

Oronten, acc. sg., according to a Greek form.

l. 114. **ipsius,** ' of (Aeneas) himself '.

vertex usually = ' head '. **a vertice** must here mean ' from above '—the ' sea ' towers above the ship's stern. **pontus** is used here, as the word ' sea ' often is in English, for a single wave.

l. 115. Take **magister** first, as subject both of **excutitur** and **volvitur. pronus** and **in caput** both go with **volvitur** : ' he is dashed out (of the ship) and falls (lit. is rolled) face downwards (and) head foremost ' (lit. ' on to his head ').

magister, ' the helmsman ', is probably Orontes himself.

l. 116. **illam,** i.e. the ship.

l. 117. **circum**, with **agens**, ' driving (her) round and round '. The two words expand **torquet**, ' rotates '.

aequore, local abl. with preposition.

vertex, like English ' vortex ' here, ' whirlpool '.

l. 118. Begin **apparent in gurgite vasto. apparent** = ' there are seen ' and has four subjects, **nantes, arma, tabulae, gaza. nantes**, nom. pl. masc. pres. partic. active of **nare**, used as a noun, ' swimmers '.

l. 119. **virum**. See note on **superum**, l. 4.

tabulae, i.e. of the shattered ship.

per, ' amid '.

l. 120. **Ilionei**, etc. These are names of some of the companions of Aeneas. Among them Achates, his closest friend, is of most importance.

ll. 120-122. A good deal is to be supplied in these three lines. The full Latin, in the order for translation, would be : **iam hiems vicit validam navem Ilionei, iam (navem) fortis Achatae, et (navem) qua Abas vectus (est) et (navem) qua grandaevus Aletes (vectus est)**. In English we should put the pronoun ' that ' in each case in which **navem** has to be supplied.

l. 121. **qua**. Latin speaks of the ship *by* which one *is carried*, we prefer to say *in* which one *sails*.

l. 122. **laxis** is for **laxatis**, ' being loosened ', and goes with **compagibus** in the abl. absolute construction : ' with the bolts of their sides loosened '.

omnes, fem., agrees with **naves** understood.

l. 123. **imbrem**, lit., ' rain ', put poetically here for ' sea '.

rimis, local abl., ' at the seams '. First the ' fastenings ' (**compages**) are loosened, then the planks gape, no longer held together.

ll. 124, 126. The order for translation is **Interea Neptunus, graviter commotus, sensit pontum misceri magno murmure, hiememque emissam (esse), et stagna refusa (esse) imis vadis**.

l. 124. **murmure.** ' Murmur ' does not represent here the meaning of the Latin word, which is often very much stronger. Say ' roaring '.

l. 125. **imis vadis,** abl. of place whence, without preposition **ab** or **ex.**

l. 126. **stagna,** ' the still waters, ' i.e. the sea at the bottom, normally not disturbed by ordinary gales ; but the present storm is supernatural, with all the winds blowing at once.

alto, probably ' over the deep ', with **prospiciens.** It is a local ablative, equivalent to **per altum.**

l. 127. **placidum.** This at first seems inconsistent with **graviter commotus,** l. 126. Vergil is however perhaps thinking of some familiar statue or picture of the god, and by his use of the word suggests that not even the passion of anger can ruffle the majestic serenity of divinity.

summa unda, same abl. as **imis vadis,** l. 125. For the adj. **summus** meaning ' surface of ' cf. l. 110.

l. 128. **toto aequore,** ' over all the sea ', local abl.

l. 129. **Troas,** acc. pl. masc., according to a Greek form. **oppressos** agrees with it.

caelique ruinā, ' and by the havoc of the sky '. **caeli** is subjective, not objective genitive, i.e. the sky (or rather the winds that fill it) is the author, not the sufferer, of the havoc. The phrase is a poetic variation, then, for **ruentibus ventis,** ' by the rushing winds '.

l. 130. **latuere,** for **latuerunt. lateo,** which occurred, l. 108, in its usual meaning, ' lurk ', ' am hidden ', is here a transitive verb, with **fratrem** as object, meaning ' elude ', ' escape the notice of '.

fratrem, i.e. Neptune.

l. 131. **dehinc,** scanned as one syllable, dēīnc.

tantane. -ne is interrogative particle, and **tanta** qualifies **fiducia.**

l. 132. **generis fiducia vestri,** ' pride of—English says ' in '—
your birth '. Certain of the winds were the children of a Titan
by Aurora, goddess of the dawn.

l. 134. **tantas moles,** ' masses so great ', i.e. ' such monstrous
waves '.

l. 135. **quos ego**—! Neptune begins a sentence apparently
containing a threat of punishment : ' whom I (will) ' and then
breaks off as a more urgent task, the undoing of the mischief,
claims his attention.

praestat. The subject is the infinitive **componere,** but in
such cases English usually begins with an anticipatory ' it '
and puts the real subject after : ' it is of more urgency to
soothe . . .'

l. 136. Probably ' hereafter you shall pay me for your
offences with a different (*lit.,* not similar) punishment ', i.e. next
time you shall be punished more severely, though this is
awkward because there has been no punishment, except
Neptune's words of rebuke. Another possible meaning is,
' afterwards (i.e. when I have calmed the waves) you shall pay
me for your offences with a disproportionate penalty ', i.e.
great as your offence has been, your punishment, when I am
at liberty to inflict it, shall be greater.

l. 137. **haec,** acc. pl. neut.

l. 138. **imperium** and **tridentem** are accusative, subject to
the infinitive **datum (esse)** in the acc. and infin. construction :
' that the sovereignty . . . was given '.

tridentem. The trident was as it were the sceptre of the
sea god.

l. 139. **sorte.** According to mythology the supremacy of the
gods Jupiter, Neptune, and Pluto over their respective spheres
in heaven, in the sea, and in the underworld was determined by
the drawing of lots.

l. 140. Observe the plural possessive, **vestras,** addressed to
Eurus, best shown in English by saying, ' your home and the
home of your friends '. **vestras** includes all the winds.

iactet and **regnet** are *jussive* subjunctives, i.e. subjunctives expressing commands : ' let Aeolus, etc.'

l. 141. **clauso** is emphatic—the condition of Aeolus' kingship is that the prison shall remain closed : ' and rule within the prison, fast shut, of the winds '. **carcere** is local ablative.

l. 142. **dicto** is abl. of comparison, depending on the comparative adv. **citius** : ' more swiftly than speech '—in less time than it takes to tell of it.

l. 144. **Cymothoë**, a sea-nymph, or Nereid. **Triton**, a son of Neptune.

adnixus belongs in grammar with Triton only, in sense with both Cymothoë and Triton : ' C. and T., heaving together . . .'

l. 145. **scopulo.** See note on **imis vadis**, l. 125.

ipse, i.e. Neptune. While his helpers succour the three vessels impaled upon the rocks (l. 108), Neptune goes to the aid of the three engulfed in the sand-banks (l. 112).

l. 146. **syrtes** is probably object both of **levat** and **aperit**. Inserting his trident below the half-buried ships, he ' lifts and opens the vast sand-banks '. The lifting causes the sand-banks to gape and release the ships.

l. 147. **rotis levibus** is abl. of the instrument, expressing the things *with which* he glides, but in English we should say rather ' on light wheels '. **levibus** : the divine chariot does not sink into the sea but skims the surface.

summas, as in ll. 110, 127.

ll. 148-153. A simile, comparing the storm and Neptune's stilling of it to a civil commotion quelled by a great man. It is interesting for a number of reasons, its descent from the divine to the human, its hint of the turbulent scenes witnessed by Vergil before the Augustan peace, the poet's contempt (like Shakespeare's) for the **ignobile vulgus,** and the regard he shows in it for the ' great man ' and his spell-binding oratory.

l. 148. Begin **ac veluti cum,** ' and just as when '.

l. 149. **animis,** abl. of cause, with **saevit,** 'is furious with anger'. **animus** in the plural often has this meaning.

l. 151. The order is **tum, si forte conspexere quem virum, gravem pietate ac meritis . . . Conspexere** = con*j*pexerunt. **quem** is from **qui** indefinite, 'some'. **gravem pietate et meritis,** lit., 'weighty owing to his uprightness and his services'. Say 'having authority by reason of', etc.

l. 153. **animos** has the same meaning as in l. 149.

l. 154. **postquam,** mostly, as here, best rendered 'when'.

aequora, object of **prospiciens.**

l. 155. **genitor,** i.e. Neptune.

caelo, abl. of *route*, 'through the sky'.

aperto, i.e. no longer covered with clouds.

invectus. The passives of **veho** and its compounds are often used, like deponent verbs, with active meaning. Thus **invectus** here = 'driving on', the perfect participle, as those of deponent verbs may do, having a present meaning.

l. 156. **curru,** an old form for **currui,** dat. sg.

volans, 'flying', is best rendered by a clause, 'as he flies'. The chariot of Neptune, represented (l. 147), as gliding on the surface of the sea, is now passing through the air.

The end of this line is a little difficult. 'Gives reins to his following chariot', which is the literal meaning, is open to the objections that one gives reins to the horses, not the vehicle, and that 'following' is a weak and meaningless epithet. The second difficulty may perhaps be met by taking **secundo** to convey that the chariot 'follows' the team in the sense that its supernatural lightness makes no demands on the horses that draw it. Hence we may render 'light' or 'swift'.

l. 157. **Aeneadae** is literally 'sons of Aeneas', the -des suffix, like the -ides of ll. 97 and 99 being the Greek patronymic ending. But the actual meaning here is 'companions of'.

quae proxima litora, i.e. **litora, quae proxima (sunt),** 'the nearest shores'. As the next line shows, these shores are those of North Africa, so that the fleet has been driven a long way from the Tyrrhenian sea, where it was sailing when the tempest began.

cursu, lit., 'with running', belongs with **petere**, and may be translated 'at speed'. The ships, in their damaged state, make what speed they can for the nearest land.

l. 158. **vertuntur.** Notice that when a Roman wished to say 'I turn' (intransitive), he used the passive, **vertor.** The active voice means 'I turn (*something*)'. The same is the case with 'change', 'roll', 'move', etc. The intransitive use of **avertit**, l. 104, is exceptional.

l. 159. **est**, standing first, often = 'there is'.

l. 160. **obiectu laterum**, 'by the projection of its sides', better, 'with its projecting sides'. Three sides of the island face open sea, the fourth faces the land. The harbour lies between the island and the mainland.

omnis ab alto. The words go with **unda**, l. 161, 'every wave from the deep'.

l. 161. **inque**, etc., lit., 'and splits itself into the retired bays'. Perhaps the meaning is that the waves are broken and parted by the cliffs of the island, and the sea flows tamely through the channels at either end into the sheltered water of the harbour. Say, 'and, parting, flows into the sheltered bay'.

ll. 162, 163. **minantur in caelum**, lit., 'threaten heavenward', a way of saying 'tower threateningly to the sky'. It is not clear whether these cliffs, and the woods of ll. 164, 165, form part of the island or of the mainland.

l. 164. **silent.** In the shelter of the harbour there is no sound of breaking waves.

tum introduces the third feature of the scene. First the great cliffs, and second the still water at their foot. Finally, apparently on the cliff tops above (**desuper**) or perhaps above the calm water of the harbour, are the woods.

silvis scaena coruscis, supply **est.** 'Then, above, there is a background with (but English says 'of') waving trees'

silvis coruscis is abl. of description, like **praestanti corpore,** l. 71. The proper meaning of **coruscus** is ' glittering '. The reference here is to the alternations of light and shade upon the moving leaves.

l. 165. **atrum nemus imminet,** lit., ' a dark wood overhangs ', or as we should say, ' there is a dark, overhanging wood '.

horrenti umbra, ' with quivering shade '. As the trees are stirred by the wind, the shadow they cast moves too.

l. 166. **fronte sub adversa,** ' beneath the (cliff)-face confronting (them) ', i.e. directly ahead of the Trojans as they enter the harbour.

antrum, supply **est,** ' (there is) a cavern '.

scopulis pendentibus, abl. of description, cf. ll. 71, 164.

pendentibus, ' hanging ', because the stone of the cavern roof is unsupported below.

l. 167. With **aquae** and **sedilia,** supply **sunt,** ' there are '.

vivo saxo, abl. of description again. The seats are said to be ' of living stone ' because they are natural shelves in the solid rock of the cave.

l. 168. **Nympharum domus.** The latter word is in apposition to **antrum,** and the phrase sounds most natural if translated immediately after l. 166.

ll. 168, 169. The water within the haven is so still that the normal precautions of mooring or anchoring are not required.

hic, i.e. in the harbour.

non is to be taken with **ulla,** the two words being equivalent to **nulla.**

l. 169. **morsu,** properly ' biting ', seems here to mean ' tooth ', i.e. the fluke of an anchor.

l. 170. **septem collectis navibus** is abl. absolute. In translating use the active participle in agreement with Aeneas : ' having collected ', etc.

l. 171. **magno amore** is abl. of cause, and goes with **egressi** : ' disembarking in a great longing '.

telluris, objective genitive—the land is the object of their longing. We say ' *for* the land '.

l. 172. **optata harena,** abl., governed by the verb **potior,** which takes either abl. or gen.

l. 173. **sale tabentes,** usually taken as ' dripping with brine '.

ll. 174-176. The first step is to kindle a fire.

l. 174. **silici.** The dative in association with the compound verb **excudo,** here expresses ' from '.

l. 175. **suscepit ignem foliis,** ' caught the fire with leaves ', i.e. sets light first to some dry dead leaves.

l. 176. **dedit** = ' put ' here.

nutrimenta, ' fuel ', twigs, etc. with which the spark, that has fastened upon the dry leaves, is now fed.

rapuitque in fomite flammam, lit., ' and in the tinder snatched a flame '. ' *From* the tinder ' we should say. The **fomes** is the dry stuff already mentioned, **folia** and **nutrimenta.** So far the fire has but smouldered. By *seizing* the right moment to blow or fan it—this is expressed by **rapuit**—Achates produces flame.

l. 177. **Cererem.** The name Ceres is here used, as often in poetry, for the thing of which she is the goddess, i.e. ' corn '. Similarly **Bacchus** is found for ' wine ', **Vulcanus** for ' fire ', etc. In the same way **Cerealia arma,** ' the weapons of Ceres ', is poetic for ' implements for bread-making '.

l. 178. **fessi rerum,** ' weary of trouble ', belongs with the understood subject of **expediunt,** ' they '. The phrase should be translated immediately after **tum,** l. 177.

receptas, ' rescued ', that is, from the salt water which has spoilt it (**corruptam undis**).

l. 179. Apparently we have to understand that the sodden grain had to be dried ' over the flames ' (**flammis**) before it could be ground.

ll. 180, 181. **et omnem . . . petit,** ' and seeks an unimpeded view, far and wide, over the sea '. **omnem prospectum,** lit., ' an entire view ', is one that extends in all directions. **pelago** is local abl.

l. 181. **si** should be taken as ' in the hope that '. **Anthea,** acc. sg., Greek form, of Antheus, who, like Capys and Caicus, is one of the companions of Aeneas. With **Anthea** agrees **quem,** which is from **qui,** indefinite adjective, and means ' some ' or ' any '. But ' in the hope that he may see some Antheus ' is unnatural in English, and perhaps we may say ' some glimpse of '.

The subjunctive **videat** can be explained as final. Vergil might have written **ut videat,** ' in order that he may see '. The substitution of **si** for **ut** suggests that the purpose—to see Antheus—is conditional upon his being there to be seen.

l. 182. **biremes.** This is properly the word for a type of war-galley, powered with two ' banks ' of oars. It is used here quite generally for ' ships '.

l. 183. **Capyn,** acc. sg. Cf. **Oronten,** l. 113.

celsis in puppibus arma Caici. puppibus is pl. for sing. By **arma** is meant primarily the shield of Caicus, naturally hung at the stern because he would himself be the helmsman. **Caici** is three syllables ($\smile$ — —).

l. 184. **tres.** Before this word English requires the insertion of ' but ' or ' only '.

litore, local abl. with **errantes,** ' on ' or ' along the shore '.

l. 186. The preposition **a** (**ab**) with the words **fronte, tergo, latere, dextrā** or **sinistrā** (**manu**) expresses ' in ' or ' on ', not ' from '.

agmen, the usual word for ' column ', i.e. troops in marching formation, here means ' line ' ; the herd is ' strung out ' as it moves grazing along the floor of a narrow valley leading to the sea.

valles, pl. for sing.

l. 187. **hic,** probably adv. of time, ' thereupon ', **i.e.** on seeing the deer.

manu. We say ' seized *in* his hand ', the Romans ' with '.

l. 188. Take **tela** (in apposition to **arcum** and **sagittas)** before **quae,** ' weapons which '.

l. 189. **ductores.** These are the three stags of l. 184.

ll. 189, 190. **capita alta ferentes cornibus arboreis,** ' carrying their heads high with branching (lit. tree-like) antlers '.

ll. 190, 191. The order is **tum miscet vulgus et omnem turbam, agens telis inter frondea nemora. vulgus** and **turbam** do not mean the same thing : **vulgus** is the rank and file of the herd, those not leaders, **turbam** suggests the straggling disorder in which all are grazing : ' the common sort and all the rabble '. The object of **agens** is ' them ', i.e. the deer, understood.

l. 192. **prius** and **quam,** here separated, make one word, for which ' before ' or ' until ' will do equally well.

victor. This noun is often used much as we should use an adverb, ' victoriously ', ' triumphantly '.

l. 193. **humi. humus** is one of the very few common nouns possessing a locative case : ' on the ground '.

fundat, aequet. The use of the subjunctive here in a *time* clause introduced by **priusquam** seems irregular, because it is not easy to see the subsidiary notion of *purpose* which alone justifies that mood in such clauses, and which is to be seen for example in such a sentence as ' I would not leave until he arrived '—**priusquam venisset.** In the present case indicatives would be more natural.

et numerum cum navibus aequet, ' and matches (their) number with (that of his) ships '.

l. 194. **partitur.** The object of this verb is ' them ' (the deer) understood. The object, when a pronoun, often has to be supplied. Cf. note on **agens,** l. 191.

in, ' among '.

ll. 195, 196. The order is **deinde dividit vina quae heros,**

bonus Acestes, onerarat cadis Trinacrio litore dederatque (eis) abeuntibus.

Acestes, a Sicilian king who had befriended Aeneas.

onerarat, the *syncopated* form of the pluperfect, for **oneraverat.** In these forms the letter *v*, and sometimes the following vowel, disappear.

quae onerarat cadis, lit., 'which he had loaded in jars ', i.e ' with which he had filled jars '. The natural construction with **onero** would be the acc. of the vessel filled, abl. of the substance with which. As a parallel to the inverted construction here Sidgwick quotes, from Burns, 'Go fetch to me a pint o' wine An' fill it in a silver tassie '.

l. 196. **litore Trinacrio,** local abl., without preposition **in.**

abeuntibus, ' depaiting ', i.e. ' at their departure '.

l. 198. The **enim** shows that the words in parenthesis modify some unexpressed thought such as **nolite desperare** : ' (do not lose heart), for we have not up till now (**ante**) been ignorant of troubles ', i.e. misfortune is no novelty to us, and we should have learned to bear it.

sumus, idiomatically translated by the English perfect. Notice that ' For three hours I *have been waiting* here ' (—and still *am waiting*) is in Latin **tres horas hic** *exspecto.*

malorum is neut. pl. of the adjective **malus** used as a noun, **mala,**·' evils ', ' troubles '.

l. 199. **o passi graviora. passi** is voc. pl. masc., perf. partic. of the deponent verb **patior,** and **graviora** is its object : ' o ye having (=who have) suffered more grievous things '.

his, supply **malis** (dat.) in the same meaning as **malorum** above.

deus. The Roman poets often used the singular of this word, without having any particular god in mind, much as we say ' Heaven ' or ' Providence '.

ll. 200-202. Aeneas reminds his companions of some of their previous troubles.

l. 200. **et,** ' both '.

Scyllaeam, from the adjective **Scyllaeus, -a, -um,** equivalent to the genitive of the noun **Scylla.** Similarly for ' of Caesar ' it is possible to write **Caesaris** or **Caesarianus.**

Scylla was a sea-monster supposed to haunt the Straits of Messina. She is represented in art as a woman to the waist, terminating in a scaly mermaid-like body with a serpent's head where the tail would be. Round her waist there is a sort of kilt, composed of the head and legs of wolves.

sonantes, with **scopulos.**

l. 201. **accestis** is a contraction for **accessistis,** from **accedo.**

et, ' also '.

Cyclopia, ' of the Cyclopes '. Cf. note on **Scyllaeam** above. The Cyclopes were a race of one-eyed giants who lived near Etna. Best known of them was Polyphemus, blinded by Odysseus (Ulysses).

l. 202. **experti,** i.e. **experti estis.**

animos. In l. 149 the pl. of this word meant ' anger '. Another of its meanings, seen here, is ' spirits ', ' courage '.

l. 203. **forsan,** etc. The subject of **iuvabit** is **meminisse,** but in such cases we usually prefer to begin with an anticipatory ' it ' : ' it will be a pleasure to recall . . .'

et, ' even '. **haec,** their present sufferings.

l. 204. **discrimina rerum,** ' critical situations ', lit., ' crises of affairs '.

l. 206. **fas,** supply **est.**

regna resurgere Troiae. The first two words are acc. and infin., and the whole is subject to **est.** ' There it is lawful that Troy's realm should rise again.'

l. 207. **vosmet.** **vos** is acc. and **-met** adds emphasis.

rebus, dative.

l. 208. **voce refert,** ' brings back with his voice ', poetic for ' speaks '. The **re-** prefix seems meaningless here.

aeger. The adjective has *concessive* force : ' (though) sick '.

l. 209. **spem vultu simulat,** lit., 'he pretends hope with his face', the meaning of which is clear enough, though we should express it differently—' puts on a look of hope '.

altum, in grammar an adjective with **dolorem,** is in sense an adverb with **premit** : ' suppresses his pain, deep in his heart '. **corde** is local abl.

l. 210. **praedae,** i.e. the seven shot deer.

l. 211. **tergora.** The word has two forms, **tergum, -i,** and **tergus, -oris,** both neuter. The usual meaning is ' back '; here it is the skin of the back, ' hide '.

costis, abl. of separation, expressing that from which something is taken.

viscera, ' flesh ' here, not in its narrower meaning of ' vitals ' to which we confine the English word viscera.

l. 212. **pars** is sometimes used in the meaning ' some ' and may then, as here, take a plural verb. It is answered by alii below, meaning ' others '.

secant. The object of this verb is **ea** (= **viscera**) understood. **Ea,** though plural, must be translated ' it ', as we rendered **viscera** above by the singular ' flesh '.

trementia, ' quivering '. The beasts are barely dead.

l. 213. **aëna,** acc. pl. neut. of **aënus,** ' of copper ', used as a noun, ' things of copper ', i.e. ' cooking-pots '.

litore, local abl.

l. 214. **victu revocant vires.** Notice the alliteration, of which Vergil is fond. **vires,** acc. pl. of **vis.** Distinguish carefully the forms of this word from those of **vir, -i,** ' man '.

fusi, from **fundo,** lit., ' poured ', here ' outstretched ', ' sprawling '. The participle agrees with ' they ', subject of **implentur.**

l. 215. **implentur.** The passive is sometimes equivalent to the active and reflexive pronoun object. Here proceed as if you had **se implent.**

Bacchi, ferinae. The genitive is used after verbs denoting filling. For **Bacchus,** ' wine ', see note on **Cererem,** l. 177.

l. 216. **ex‸mpta, i.e. exempta est ;** similarly **remotae = remotae sunt.**

mensae remotae. At Roman meals ' tables ' were set beside diners ; *we* seat our guests at table. Naturally then the **mensa** was light and easily moved, and no doubt the board from which these shipwrecked sailors ate their picnic meal was some makeshift article.

l. 217. **longo sermone requirunt,** lit., ' in long converse they miss ' ; as we might say, ' tell each other at length how much they miss '.

l. 218. The order is **dubii** (' hesitating ') **inter spemque metumque.** To our minds the first **-que** (=' both ') is redundant.

seu, and (l. 219) **sive.** These words should be **utrum, an,** for the clauses are alternative indirect questions, depending on **dubii,** not alternative conditions, for which **sive** and **seu** are proper introductions.

ll. 218, 219. Beginning at **seu** a close translation is, ' whether they should suppose that (they) are alive, or are suffering the last things and do not now hear, having been called '. Say ' whether to suppose them living, or suffering extinction, and no longer hearing when called upon '.

eos must be supplied as subject to **vivere. Credant** is indirect deliberative subjunctive. The direct question would be **quid credamus,** ' what are we to believe ? '

l. 220. **pius Aeneas. pius** is Vergil's favourite adjective for Aeneas. It may be rendered ' good ', but more particularly suggests that Aeneas is ruled by a sense of duty. See note on l. 10.

Oronti, irregular genitive of **Orontes.**

l. 221. **secum,** ' inwardly ', with **gemit.**

l. 222. **Gyan,** acc. sg. Cf. **Oronten,** l. 113.

l. 223. **finis,** ' the end '—of the meal and the subsequent lamentation for lost comrades.

aethere summo, abl. of place whence without preposition **ex.**

l. 224. **velivolum.** This adjective, made up of .**velum** and **volare,** is more usually an epithet of ships, ' sail-winged '.

iacentes, lit., ' lying ' ; say ' outspread '.

l. 225. **latos,** ' wide ', i.e. ' widely dwelling ', covering great areas.

sic, ' thus ', i.e. ' as he looked '.

vertice =**in vertice,** local abl. without preposition.

constitit, defixit, indicatives in inverse **cum** clause. The clause is only technically subordinate, in sense principal.

l. 226. **lumina,** often used in poetry for ' eyes '.

regnis =**in regna,** ' upon the realms '.

ll. 227-229. The grammatical order for translation is **atque Venus, tristior et suffusa nitentes oculos lacrimis, adloquitur illum, iactantem tales curas pectore.** But it is better to keep the order of the Latin, which puts the object, **illum,** first : ' and to him . . . Venus speaks '.

l. 227. **iactantem,** ' pondering ' ; say ' as he ponders '.

l. 228. **tristior,** ' sadder (than she was before) ' and so, ' saddened '.

lacrimis oculos suffusa nitentes, ' her shining eyes suffused with tears '. The simplest way to explain the accusative **oculos,** associated with the passive participle **suffusa,** is to regard it as an instance of the accusative of respect (accusative of the part concerned) like **feminae nudae bracchia,** ' women bare as-to-the-arms '. In this case then **suffusa oculos** is ' suffused as to the eyes '.

l. 229. **qui,** the antecedent is **tu** understood : ' **o** thou who . . .'

res, ' affairs ', i.e. ' lives '.

l. 230. **rĕgis,** verb. Contrast **rēgis,** gen. sg. of **rex.**

imperiis, pl. for sg.

terres. Supply pronoun object—**eos** (=**homines et deos**). Cf. ll. 191, 194 for other examples of similar omission.

l. 231. **meus Aeneas.** He was the son of Venus by a mortal father, Anchises. Aeneas is subject to **potuit,** to be supplied from **potuere** (=**potuerunt**) following.

tantum belongs with **quid,** ' what (crime) so grave '.

l. 232. Take **committere** again with **potuere.**

quibus is dative, and **passis** agrees with it : ' to whom, having suffered ', i.e. ' after suffering '.

funera. funus, ' funeral ', is often used for ' death '.

l. 233. **terrarum orbis.** The phrase is the normal Latin for ' the world '. Remember that **orbis** is a circle or disc, not a sphere.

ob Italiam. ob here =' for the sake of '. To prevent them from settling in Italy, Venus says, they are being prevented from settling anywhere.

ll. 234-237. The order is **certe pollicitus (es) hinc, volventibus annis, Romanos olim fore, hinc ductores a revocato sanguine Teucri, qui tenerent mare, qui (tenerent) omnes terras dicione** After **pollicitus es** acc. and infin. construction follows. Begin, ' Assuredly thou didst promise that . . .'

hinc, ' hence ', ' from this source ', i.e. ' from them '—Aeneas and his Trojans.

volventibus annis, abl. abs., ' with the years rolling (on) ', i.e. ' in the course of years '. **volvo** is here used intransitively. It normally means ' I roll (something) '.

olim, ' some day '.

fore, ' should be ', i.e. ' should arise '.

revocato, ' restored ', ' renewed '.

Teucri. Teucer was a Trojan king.

qui . . . tenerent, ' to hold '. Final clauses are often introduced by the relative pronoun, instead of by **ut,** when there is a suitable antecedent.

l. 238. **hoc,** abl., ' with this (promise) '.

solabar, here literally ' mitigated ' ; say ' consoled myself for '.

l. 239. **fatis contraria fata rependens,** i.e. comforting herself for the doom which had overtaken Troy by dwelling on the splendid destiny promised to Troy's Roman descendants. The grammar is ' weighing fates contrary to fates '.　Say ' balancing the one destiny with the other so different '.

l. 240. **eadem,** ' same '—as before.

fortuna, ' ill fortune '.

actos, participle with concessive force, ' (though) harassed '. Their past trials alone warrant a change of fortune, apart from the pledge given by Jupiter.

ll. 242-249. Venus expostulates at the superior fortune of another Trojan, Antenor, who has successfully established himself in the Italian peninsula already.

l. 242. **mediis Achivis,** abl. of separation dependent on **elapsus. Achivi** is properly the name for the people of a part of Greece ; here, and very often, it stands for ' the Greeks ' as a whole.

l. 243. **Illyricos.** Illyricum lay to the east of the Adriatic forming part of what we now call Jugo-Slavia.　Perhaps **Illyricos sinus penetrare,** ' to thread the Illyrian gulfs ' suggests a voyage up the eastern coast of the Adriatic following the channels between the very numerous islands.

tutus, adj. for adv., ' safely '.

l. 244. **regna,** also governed by **penetrare.**

Liburnorum. Their territory lay in what we now know as Croatia.

Timavi. This is a little river that enters the sea in the Gulf of Trieste.　For part of its course it flows underground.　It is not clear whether the next two lines mean that the river over-

flows and covers the surrounding land with a sea-like flood,
or that the sea actually enters the underground channel and
pours up through holes in the ground. Perhaps the first is
more natural, in which case ll. 245, 246 will run : 'whence,
through nine mouths, while the mountain thunders loudly,
there issues (it) a rushing sea and covers the fields with a roaring
flood '.

With **vasto cum murmure montis**, lit., 'with the vast
thunder of the mountain ', cf. the similar phrase in l. 55.
Probably in the present line the allusion is to the noise pro·
duced by the river in its passage through underground channels
below the mountain.

l. 247. **hic**, adv.

ille, Antenor.

urbem Patavi. **Patavi** = **Patavii**, gen. of **Patavium**, the modern
Padua, inland from Venice, the fourth and final stage of
Antenor's journey after **sinus Illyrici, regna Liburnorum,** and
fons Timavi. The more usual Latin for ' city of Padua '
would be **urbs Patavium,** with both nouns in the same case.

sedesque. Drop the -**que** and proceed as if **sedes** were in
apposition to **urbem**. Such an insertion of ' and ' is not
uncommon.

l. 248. **Teucrorum**. English would say ' *for* the Trojans '.

fixit, ' has hung up '—in temples. He is at peace.

l. 249. **Troia**, 3 syllables. It is from the adjective **Troius,**
-**a, -um**, and agrees with **arma**.

compostus = **compositus**, ' settled '.

ll. 250-253. How different from Antenor's is the treatment
we receive—I and my son Aeneas, whose deserts are greater.

l. 250. **nos**. Venus by her ' we ' means herself and Aeneas.

tua progenies. According to one of the various myths about
the birth of Venus, she was the daughter of Jupiter. Aeneas,
then, her son, can equally with his mother be termed **Iovi·
progenies**.

caeli quibus adnuis arcem. Jove has promised Aeneas a place in Olympus.

adnuis, historic present.

l. 251. **navibus amissis,** abl. abs. But it is a case similar though not exactly parallel to that commented on in l. 69— i.e. participle replacing finite verb. Proceed as if you had **naves amisimus et.**

infandum, acc. of exclamation : ' a shameful thing! '

unius, supply **deae.** Juno is meant.

l. 252. **Italis oris,** abl. of separation.

l. 253. **hic pietatis honos?** supply **est. Hic** is emphatic : ' Is *this* the reward . . . '

sic, too, is emphatic : ' (is it) *thus* (that) thou restorest . . . ? ' Notice that it is necessary to insert three words in order to secure this emphasis.

in sceptra, ' to power ', the pl. being used for the sing., and the *symbol* of power for power itself.

l. 254. **olli** is an old form of **illi,** dat. sg. Vergil is fond of old-fashioned words and forms, a fondness which has been characteristic of much English poetry, too.

l. 255. **vultu quo,** ' with (that) look with which '.

l. 256. **oscula libavit natae. libo** here = ' kiss ', usually ' taste '.

dehinc, scanned as one syllable.

l. 257. **metu** is an old form of the dative singular. ' Spare thy fear ' is of course equivalent to ' Fear not '.

Cytherea, voc. The name is one of the titles of Venus, and is derived from Cythera, an island, lying off the southern coast of the Peloponnese, where the goddess was particularly worshipped.

tuorum, masc. pl., ' of thy (people) '—i.e. Aeneas and his Trojans.

l. 258. **Lavini** = **Lavinii.** The gen. sg. of nouns in **-ius** and

-ium will be found in both these forms. Lavinium was the name of the capital of the kingdom which was founded later by Aeneas in Italy.

l. 259. **feres ad sidera caeli,** i.e. you will make a god of him. **sublimem,** in grammar an adjective with **Aenean,** is to be taken closely with the verb : ' bear aloft '.

Aenean, acc. sg., Greek form.

l. 260. **vertit,** probably perfect.

l. 261. **hic,** i.e. Aeneas.

fabor, from **for.**

quando here means ' since ', in the causal, not the temporal sense.

l. 262. **et volvens,** etc., ' and, (un)rolling (them), will reveal the secrets of fate '. The metaphor derives from the ancient form of book (**volumen**), a scroll mounted at each end on wooden sticks.

l. 263. **geret.** The subject is Aeneas—the **hic** of l. 261.

Italiā, i.e. in Italia.

l. 264. **ponet.** If the verb be translated ' shall establish ' the awkwardness (to English minds) of its being used in two different senses, metaphorically with **mores,** literally with **moenia,** will disappear.

ll. 265, 266. The reign of Aeneas will last three years.

l. 265. **dum,** ' until '.

regnantem agrees with **eum** understood.

videri is fut. perf. English idiom, less correctly, prefers the perfect.

Latio. Cf. Italia, l. 263.

l. 266. **terna.** The distributive numeral, here properly meaning ' three *each* ', is often used in poetry for the cardinal. Translate ' three '.

hiberna. With this adjective **tempora** is apparently to be understood. **Tempora hiberna** then = **hiemes,** ' winters '.

Rutulis subactis, probably dative, in association with **transierint :** ' have passed over for the subdued Rutulians '. In translation we should drop the ' for '.

Rutulis. These were an Italian tribe. Their chief, Turnus, was the leader of native opposition to the settlement of the Trojans in Italy and to the marriage of Aeneas with Lavinia, daughter of King Latinus.

ll. 267-271. Ascanius, the son of Aeneas, shall reign for 30 years and build a new capital.

l. 267. **Iulo.** Notice that the name has been attracted into the case of the relative pronoun **cui,** and compare **volitans cui nomen asilo Romanum est,** ' a winged insect, for which the Roman name is asilus '. In the English rendering ' to whom the surname Iulus is now added ', ' Iulus ' is nominative in apposition to ' surname '.

It was from this Iulus that the Julian family, to which Augustus belonged, liked to trace their descent.

l. 268. **stetit regno,** ' stood in sovereignty '.

ll. 269, 270. **triginta . . . explebit,** ' shall complete with his rule (—say ' as ruler ') thirty great circles with (our idiom is ' of ') rolling months ', i.e. shall reign for 30 years.

volvendis mensibus. The ablative is one of description, like **praestanti corpore,** l. 71, and as in that case must be rendered by a phrase with ' of '. The gerundive **volvendus** has here the force of an *intransitive* present participle, **volvens,** the usual participle, being strictly transitive only.

l. 270. **ab sede Lavini,** lit., ' from its seat of Lavinium '. This we should express differently, either by ' its seat, Lavinium ' or ' its seat *at* Lavinium '. For the form of the genitive cf. l. 258.

l. 271. **longam Albam.** Alba Longa was the second capital of the Trojan exiles and the Italian peoples with whom they mingled.

l. 272. **hic,** adverb.

iam, ' henceforth ', ' from that time on '.

regnabitur. An example of an important idiom of Latin, the impersonal passive, by which a verb in the 3rd person singular passive is used to express action on the part of an indefinite subject, much as the French use ' on ' and the English ' they '. A very familiar example, to those who have read some Caesar, is **pugnatum est,** ' they fought ', ' there was fighting ', etc. **regnabitur** then = ' there will be ruling ', and we may render ' the kingdom will continue '.

l. 273. **Hectorea,** i.e. ' Trojan ', Hector, as the greatest soldier of Troy, standing for the people as a whole.

ll. 274, 275. **donec,** etc. The order is **donec Ilia, sacerdos regina, gravis Marte, dabit partu geminam prolem.**

Ilia was a descendant of Aeneas. Another name for her is Rhea Silvia.

regina is best rendered as an adjective here, ' royal '.

l. 274. **dabit partu,** ' shall give at a birth '. Our idiom is ' shall give birth to '.

geminam prolem. The ' twin offspring ' are Romulus and Remus.

l. 275. Begin **inde, Romulus, laetus fulvo tegmine lupae, nutricis . . .**

laetus tegmine, lit., ' joyful in the hide '. **tegmine** is abl. of cause, telling *why* he is joyful. Render **laetus** ' proudly wearing '.

lupae nutricis. The reference is to the story that the twins, after being exposed to die by their uncle, were found and suckled by a she-wolf.

l. 276. **excipiet,** lit., ' shall take over from another '. Say ' shall next reign over '.

Mavortia. Mavors is another name of the god Mars. The walls of Rome are called ' Martian ' because built by Romulus, son of Mars.

l. 277. **Romanos** agrees with **homines,** understood, readily enough, from **gentem.**

dicet. The verb here means 'call'.

l. 278. 'For these (people) I appoint neither goals nor seasons of empire' (**rerum**). **meta,** properly a pylon marking the turning-point in a race course, is a limit in space, **tempus,** a limit in time. Roman power, says Jove, is to be world-wide and eternal. For the meaning of **rerum** in this sentence cf. l. 268.

l. 280. **metu,** abl. of cause, 'in her fear'. What Juno fears is the rise of a new Troy.

fatigat, 'wearies' them, that is, by the turmoil she has caused in them.

l. 281. **in melius,** as we say, 'for the better'. **melius** is acc. sg. neut. of the comparative adjective.

l. 282. **rerum,** 'of (all) things', i.e. 'of the world'.

gentemque. Ignore the -que. In Latin, a noun which to our minds should be in apposition to another is sometimes connected with it by a conjunction.

l. 283. **sic placitum,** supply **est fatis,** 'thus it has pleased the fates', i.e. 'so it has been decreed'. **Placeo** uses as perfects **placui** and **placitus sum,** both with active meaning.

lustris labentibus, abl. absolute, 'with the years gliding', i.e. 'as the years roll on'. **lustrum** properly means a period of five years.

ll. 284, 285. One day the Trojans shall triumph over the Greeks.

l. 284. **domus Assaraci.** Assaracus was a king of Troy and an ancestor of Aeneas, so 'the house of Assaracus' is a poetic way of saying the race founded by Aeneas.

Phthiam. A town of Greece, selected to represent Greece as a whole because it was the birthplace of Achilles, the noblest champion of the Greeks who fought at Troy. Mycenae and Argos are chosen for similar reasons, the first having been the city of Agamemnon, leader of the expedition against Troy, and the second of Diomedes, another Greek prominent in the war.

l. 285. **servitio premet,** 'shall enslave' will do for the two words—lit., 'shall crush with slavery'.

Argis. Vergil here makes this place a 2nd decl. masc. pl. noun. It is called in English Argos. The case of **Argis** is probably local abl., 'in . . . Argos', rather than dat. of disadvantage, 'over Argos', because of another Vergilian line **unde genus Longa nostrum dominabitur Alba** (VI, 766), where there is no doubt of the case.

ll. 286-288. The order is **nascetur** ('there shall be born') **pulchra origine Troianus Caesar, qui terminet imperium Oceano, famam astris, Iulius, nomen demissum a magno Iulo.**

l. 286. **pulchra origine,** 'of noble lineage'. With **nascor** an abl. of the source from which, called abl. of origin, is often found.

Troianus. Caesar is called Trojan because, according to the family legend, the Iulii sprang from Iulus, the son of Aeneas.

l. 287. 'to end his sovereignty (only) at Ocean, his glory at the stars', i.e. wherever there is land, he shall rule, wherever there is space, he shall be known. **terminet** is final subjunctive, with **qui** replacing **ut is.** This is the purpose of Caesar's being born. **Oceano** and **astris are** really abls. of the instrument, what he is to limit his sway and fame *with*.

l. 288. **olim,** 'one day'—in the future ; more often it relates to past time, and means 'formerly', 'once upon a time'. It is an adverb derived from **ille.** Compare the archaic dative **olli,** which occurs l. 254.

caelo, 'in heaven'.

spoliis Orientis onustum. This phrase, and the first part of l. 294, make it clear that the **Caesar** of l. 286, who is to be admitted to heaven, is not the dictator Julius, but his adopted son Octavius, who according to Roman custom was known after his adoption as Caius Iulius Caesar Octavianus, most familiar to us under his title of Augustus. The words 'laden with the spoils of the East' refer to his victory over Cleopatra of Egypt, a recent memory to his protégé Vergil when the latter was writing the Aeneid.

l. 289. **secura** agrees with **tu**: ' him . . . shalt thou welcome, freed from anxiety '.   The disquiet that Venus now feels regarding the future of her favourite Aeneas and his descendants will pass with the reception into heaven of Augustus.

l. 290. **quoque,** i.e. like Aeneas, or any other god.   Julius and Augustus, and other Roman emperors, were worshipped as gods after their death, and sometimes, by their Oriental subjects, while yet living.

l. 291. **positis bellis,** abl. absolute.   **pono** has the meaning here of ' put *down* ', ' lay *aside* '.   Begin ' then, with wars at an end . . .'   Under Augustus the Pax Romana has begun. His greatest claim on the affections of the ancient world was that he had brought to an end an era of bitter civil wars, the misery of which Vergil had experienced and well remembered.

l. 292. **cana,** properly ' white-haired ', and so ' ancient '. **Fides,** ' honour ' had been a feature of earlier Roman character. Vergil means that Augustus will bring back the good faith, long since corrupted, of a nobler period of Roman history.

Vesta was the Roman goddess of fire.   She is mentioned here for the antiquity of her worship, and the fact that hers was a native cult, not a foreign importation.

Quirinus is another name of Romulus.   In mentioning Romulus and Remus as joint law-givers Vergil is saying poetically that there will be no more civil wars, for according to the story the brothers had quarrelled and Remus was slain by Romulus.

ll. 293, 294. ' Terrible with their close-fitting iron fastenings, the gates of War shall be shut '.

dirae is something of a transferred epithet, fitting ' war ' better than ' gates '.

ferro et compagibus, lit., ' with iron and fastenings ' is an example of hendiadys.   Cf. note on l. 54.

Here **ferro et** is put for **ferreis.**

Belli portae. The reference is to the temple of Janus, a Roman god of war. His temple was closed in time of peace, and had been shut only three times in Roman history, for the third time by Augustus.

l. 294. **Furor impius,** 'fratricidal Rage'. **Furor** is personified blood-lust, and is called **impius,** 'contrary to duty', 'unnatural', because it is the spirit of *civil* war that Vergil has in mind.

intus, in the closed temple of war.

ll. 295, 296. **vinctus post tergum,** lit., 'bound behind his back'. The picture is clear though the expression is strange. Say 'with his hands bound behind his back,' as if the Latin were **manibus post tergum vinctis.**

l. 296. **horridus,** adj. for adv., 'horribly'.

l. 297. **Maiā genitum,** lit., 'the (one) born of Maia', i.e. 'the son of Maia'. This is Mercury, the messenger of the gods. **Maia** is abl. of origin. See note on **origine,** l. 286.

ab alto. alto is neut. sg. of the adjective used as a noun, much as English uses 'deep' for 'sea'. Translate 'from on high'.

l. 299. **hospitio Teucris,** lit., 'for hospitality to the Trojans', i.e. 'to welcome the T.'. **hospitio** is the dative of purpose, like **excidio,** l. 22.

fati is a good example of the objective genitive, bearing as it does the same relation to **nescia** as object does to verb in the sentence **fatum nescit.**

l. 300. **finibus,** abl. of separation, 'from . . .'

arceret. The object is **eos** (=**Teucros**) understood. Note the tense of **arceret** and cf. **pateant** above. After **demittit,** a historic present, either primary or historic sequence would be in order, and here we have each in turn.

aëra. Distinguish this, the acc. sg. of **aër,** 'air', from **aera,**

nom. voc. acc. pl. of **aes**, ' copper '. This acc. sg. ending in **-a** occurs in nouns derived from Greek.

l. 301. **remigio alarum**, lit., ' with the oarage of his wings ', a poetical phrase, taken by Vergil from a Greek poet, for ' on his propelling wings '.

citus, adj. for adv.

oris. Whether **oris** is dat., or local ablative, the sense is plain, ' upon the shores '.

l. 303. **corda**. **Cor** is sometimes the physical ' heart ', sometimes the seat of thought, ' mind '. The meaning here is ' thoughts '.

volente deo, ' with the god willing ', abl. abs., i.e. ' by the will of God '.

l. 304. **in** here means ' towards '.

l. 306. **ut primum**, ' when first ' = ' as soon as '.

data est, ' was vouchsafed '. Take **constituit**, l. 309, immediately after this clause. The four infinitives **exire, explorare, quaerere, referre** depend on it.

ll. 306, 307. **locos novos**. ' New places ' is too bald—say ' his strange surroundings '.

ll. 307, 308. The three indirect questions **quas . . . oras, qui (eas) teneant, hominesne feraene (sint)** are the objects of **quaerere**, which must be translated before them : ' to investigate to what shores he has come with the wind ', etc.

l. 307. **oras**. The simple accusative after **accedo** is poetic. In prose **ad** is usually employed.

vento accesserit. This is neater if turned ' the wind has brought him '. The subjunctive **accesserit** (and **teneant**, next line) is due to the indirect question. **Vento** is an abl. of the instrument.

l. 308. **teneant**. Supply **eas** (= **oras**) as object.

inculta. **incultas** would have been more correct, with **eas** and **esse** to be supplied : ' for he sees that t'ey are untilled '.

hominesne feraene. Supply **sint,** and note that **feraene** is put for **an ferae,** 'whether they are men or beasts'.

l. 309. **exacta,** lit., 'the completed things', i.e. 'the tidings', the results of his exploration.

l. 310. **in convexo nemorum,** lit., 'in a vault of woods', must mean 'beneath a roof of overarching boughs'. We must assume an arm of the harbour, narrow enough for the trees upon its shores to interweave their branches overhead. Beneath this concealment Aeneas hides the fleet—his ships were few and small. **convexo,** properly abl. sg. neut. of the participle **convexus,** 'arched', 'concave', is used here as a noun, 'vault', as was **altum,** l. 297, for 'sky'.

sub, apparently 'at the foot of'. The usual meaning 'under' seems unlikely after **in convexo nemorum.**

l. 311. **horrentibus umbris,** see note, l. 165.

l. 312. **ipse,** Aeneas.

uno = solo.

l. 313. **bina,** for **duo,** like **terna** for **tria,** l. 266.

lato hastilia ferro, 'spears with broad iron', means 'broad-bladed spears'.

l. 314. Latin is fond of beginning sentences, even after a full stop, with a relative pronoun. This is contrary to our practice and we should say 'to him', not 'to whom'.

sese tulit obvia, 'presented herself', lit., 'brought herself in his way'. **obvia** is nom., agreeing with the subject of **tulit.** More naturally Vergil might have written **obviam** agreeing with **sese.**

media silva, i.e. **in media silva.**

l. 315. It is not easy to find a translation for **gerens** that will fit equally well its three objects **os, habitum** and **arma,** since neither 'wearing' nor 'bearing' will do in every case. Say with ', or 'having '.

l. 316. **Spartanae.** At Sparta girls shared the martial sports of the boys.

ll. 316, 317. Comparisons introduced by **qualis are** liable to be very condensed. If everything required by strict grammar were inserted we should have, in translation order **vel (arma talis virginis) qualis (est) Threissa Harpalyce (quae) fatigat equos praevertiturque fugā volucrem Hebrum.** Say, ' or those of such a one as Thracian Harpalyce who˙. . .', etc.

l. 316. **Threissa.** Thrace is now European Turkey and Bulgaria.

l. 317. **fatigat,** by out-running them.

Harpalyce, a princess of Thrace and a famous huntress.

fugā, ' in flight '.

Hebrum. This is a Thracian river, now the Maritza, called **volucris,** ' winged ', because of its rapid flow.

l. 319. **venatrix** is in apposition with the subject of **suspenderat** : ' she, a huntress '. Our idiom is ' huntress-like '.

diffundere. This use of the infinitive to indicate the purpose of an action, ' had given her hair to the winds *to scatter* ' is not a common Latin idiom, but is more frequent in Greek, and we have to remember that Vergil (and the other Latin poets) were so steeped in the literature of Greece that they tended, perhaps unconsciously, to introduce into their Latin fashions of speech less characteristic of their own tongue than of Greek.

However, grammarians believe that the infinitive of both languages was originally the dative case of a verbal noun, so that **diffundere** is properly ' for spreading out '.

l. 320. ' with knee bare, and her flowing robe gathered in a knot ', lit., ' bare as to the knee '—**genu** being accusative of respect, like **oculos,** l. 228—' and having gathered her flowing robes in a knot '.

collecta. Note the active meaning of this passive participle, governing the direct object **sinus fluentes.** This is another importation from Greek, being an imitation of the ' middle ' voice of that language, which, while having most of its forms identical with those of the passive, has the active meaning of doing something to or for oneself. Compare **inutile ferrum**

cingitur, 'he *girds upon himself* his useless sword'. We call such instances in Latin the 'middle use of the passive voice'.

l. 321. **prior,** i.e. Venus opens the conversation. For **ac prior inquit,** say 'and she was the first to speak, saying . . .'

monstrate, practically = ' tell me ', here.

l. 322. The order is **si forte vidistis quam mearum sororum errantem hic. quam,** from the *indefinite* pronoun **quis,** means ' any ' or ' one '.

l. 324. **cursum prementem,** 'pressing the course' is 'following hard upon the track'.

l. 325. **Sic Venus,** supply **locuta est.**

orsus, i.e. **orsus est** (from **ordior**).

l. 326. **audita,** i.e. **audita est.**

mihi, ' by me '. This is usually called the dative of the agent, and is not uncommon after a passive participle. It is also the usual way of expressing ' by . . .' after a gerundive : **Caesari omnia uno tempore erant agenda,** ' Everything had to be done by Caesar at once '.

l. 327. **memorem,** the deliberative subjunctive used in questions to express uncertainty as to one's course of action, e.g. **quid faciam,** ' what am I to do? ' So **quam te memorem** is ' what am I to call thee? '

haud tibi (est), ' there is not to thee ', i.e. ' thou hast not '. **Tibi** is the dative of the possessor.

l. 328. **nec vox hominem sonat,** lit., ' nor does thy voice sound man ', which plainly means ' sound human ', the noun **hominem** being put where we should expect an adjective, **humanum** or **mortale.**

l. 329. **an** sometimes introduces single questions, much as **-ne** might do. In this line the verb **es** must be twice supplied.

l. 330. **sis** and **leves** are jussive subjunctives, equivalent in meaning to imperatives, except that they are perhaps more deferential in tone.

felix, usually ' lucky ', is more akin to ' luck-bringing ' here. Say ' be kind '.

quaecumque. Supply **es** again.

ll. 331, 332. The order is **et doceas tandem sub quo caelo, in quibus oris orbis, iactemur.**

tandem, usually ' at length ', sometimes has in commands or questions the force of the English ' pray '.

doceas, same subjunctive as **sis** and **leves** above.

iactemur, subjunctive in indirect question. Remember that any noun clause introduced by an interrogative word is an indirect question : the verb on which it depends need not be one of asking.

iactemur seems to mean ' we are afflicted ', ' we suffer affliction '. The more literal sense ' toss about ' is not appropriate when the fleet is safe in harbour and the speaker himself ashore.

l. 332. **locorum.** The plural of **locus** is equivalent to the English singular ' country '. ' Places ' would be intolerable as a translation here.

l. 333. **acti** agrees with the subject of **erramus.**

l. 334. **multa,** ' many *a* '.

nostra dextra is poetically put for **mea manu.**

l. 335. **tali honore.** The construction of the verb **dignor** is accusative of the person, ablative of the thing : ' deem *myself* worthy *of such tribute* '. The ablative similarly accompanies the adjective **dignus.**

l. 337. i.e. to wear high hunting-boots.

l. 338. **regna,** pl. for sg.

Agenoris. He was a king of Phoenicia, and therefore colonists from Tyre are poetically called his sons.

l. 339. **fines Libyci (sunt),** ' our frontiers (are) Libyan '.

genus is in loose apposition to the adjective **Libyci,** an ungrammatical yet comprehensible construction, as if **finitimi sunt Libyes,** ' our neighbours are Libyans ' had preceded.

l. 340. **imperium regit** means ' is our queen ', more literally ' controls the power '.

Tyria, as the scansion will show, is ablative, and **urbe = ab urbe.**

l. 341. **longa est iniuria.** By **iniuria,** ' ill-treatment ', Vergil means ' the *story of her* wrongs '.

l. 342. **ambages,** ' a roundabout way ', i.e. ' the winding course '—of the story of Dido's wrongs.

l. 342. **summa,** etc. ' I will trace (lit., follow) the chief features of the tale '. **fastigium** is that which is highest, a peak, summit—in a narrative the points of greatest importance. Notice the wide variety of meaning, according to context, which **res** can bear, and the indifference with which singular and plural can be used.

l. 343. **huic.** Translate this as if **huius,** ' her ', were read. The grammar is ' to her the husband was Sychaeus ', and **huic** is the dative of the possessor.

ll. 343, 344. **agri Phoenicum.** Both genitives depend on **ditissimus** : ' richest of the Phoenicians in land '. The genitive **agri** is similar to that which normally accompanies **plenus,** ' full '.

l. 344. **miserae.** Better taken as dative than genitive. The dative is that of the agent, like **mihi** in l. 326, and the translation ' by the unhappy girl '.

l. 345. **cui.** The antecedent is **Sychaeus,** but in English it is more natural to begin a new sentence here and say for **cui,** ' to him '.

intactam is equivalent to a noun, **virginem,** here. Dido, of course, is meant, and **pater** is ' her father '.

ll. 345, 346. **primis ominibus.** As the taking of omens was an accompaniment of marriage this phrase is equivalent to ' in her first bridals '.

iugarat, a syncopated form, is for **iugaverat.** Both its direct object and indirect object (**eam ei**) need to be supplied.

l. 346. **regna.** See note, l. 338.

l. 347. **scelere,** abl. of respect, going with **immanior.** Cf. note, l. 72.

ante here = **quam,** ' than '.

l. 348. **quos** is governed by **inter,** and should be translated ' them ', since the beginning of new sentences with the relative pronoun is unnatural in English.

medius may be ignored. It practically repeats **inter.**

venit furor, i.e. they quarrelled.

ille, Pygmalion.

ll. 348-351. **ille . . . germanae.** Observe how packed with detail this is. The one verb **superat** is modified by no less than seven adverbial expressions, four of which are actually adjectival in grammar and agree with subject or object : **impius, ante aras** (tells where and moreover explains **impius**) **auri caecus amore** (tells the motive) **clam** (the manner) **ferro** (the instrument) **incautum** (tells why the attempt succeeded) **securus amorum germanae** (adds the detail that he had no regard for his sister's happiness). We may render, adapting the order, ' Blinded by greed of gold, and heedless of his sister's love, he secretly slew with the sword the unsuspecting Sychaeus, impiously, before the altars '.

auri is objective genitive, dependent on **amore. amorum,** l. 350, is similar.

amore, abl. of cause, going with **caecus,** lit., ' blind owing to love '.

ll. 350, 351. The two adjectives **aegram** and **amantem,** ' sick ' and ' loving ', inevitably suggest ' the love-sick bride '.

l. 352. **multa simulans,** lit., ' pretending many things ', i.e. ' by many pretences '.

malus, adj. for adv., ' wickedly '.

l. 353. Begin with **sed.**

in somnis, ' in *her* (=Dido's) sleep '.

inhumati. The ghost of an unburied corpse would be particularly liable to walk.

l. 354. **ora,** pl. for sg.

modis miris, abl. of manner, and pl. for sg., 'in wondrous wise'.

l. 356. **nudavit,** 'bared' in the sense of 'made known'.

caecum. This word, usually 'blind', 'unseeing', has sometimes, as here, the meaning 'unseen', 'hidden'.

domūs, gen.

l. 357. **celerare, excedere.** A prose writer would have expressed these indirect petitions by **ut celeret, ut excedat,** instead of by the infinitive.

The literal translation of **celerare fugam,** 'to hasten flight' can hardly express the poet's meaning, for it would imply that Dido was in flight already. Say 'to fly in haste'.

patria, abl. of place whence, dependent on **excedere.**

l. 358. **auxilium viae,** lit., 'a help of the way', with **auxilium** in apposition to **thesauros.** Plain apposition is very common in Latin where the corresponding English usage is to connect the nouns with 'as'. '(As) a help of the way' means 'to help her on her way'.

tellure, probably for **e tellure.**

thesauros, singular in English.

l. 359. **ignotum,** not 'unknown' in the sense of 'unweighed,' but = 'of which none knew'.

l. 360. **his,** supply **verbis.**

fugam sociosque parabat. It is awkward in English to have two direct objects of such different types dependent on the same verb. It is perhaps best to translate the verb twice : 'prepared for flight and secured companions (to share it)'.

l. 361. **quibus.** As often, the antecedent (here **ei**) must be supplied : '(those) assemble to whom there was . . .', i.e. 'who had . . .' **quibus** is dative of the possessor again, like **tibi,** l. 327.

tyranni, objective genitive.

l. 362. **naves,** acc. pl.

paratae, supply **sunt.**

l. 364. **Pygmalionis opes.** It is not clear whether 'the riches of P.' means additional treasure already belonging to the king, or that of the dead Sychaeus which he had come to regard as his own.

pelago might be a poetic dative, ' to the sea ' (for loading in the ships). Perhaps it is better taken as local ablative, ' over the sea '.

dux femina facti, ' the leader of the exploit (is) a woman '. Dido, in spite of her sex, directs all.

l. 365. **locos,** for **ad locos,** the poetic accusative of the goal of motion. Cf. **Italiam,** l. 2.

cernes, mind the tense.

l. 367. **mercati,** i.e. **mercati sunt.**

facti de nomine Byrsam ' (called) Byrsa, after the name of their deed '. According to the story of the foundation of Carthage, the citadel, Byrsa, was so called because the natives had agreed to give the colonists as much land as a bull's hide (in Greek *bursa*) would cover, whereupon the hide was cut into very thin strips which, knotted together, enclosed an area much greater than the natives had intended to concede. The legend arose from the Greeks' confusing their own word *bursa* with the Phoenician name *bosra,* meaning ' citadel '.

l. 368. **quantum,** i.e. **tantum quantum,** ' as much as ', object of **mercati sunt. possent,** subjunctive because the clause *reports* part of the words of the concession made by the natives, **licet vobis solum mercari quantum poteritis** . . . Grammarians call such partial reportings cases of ' virtual oratio obliqua.'

l. 369. **sed vos qui tandem ?** i.e., **sed qui tandem estis vos ?** with **tandem** having the same meaning as in l. 331.

quibus aut. Take **aut** first.

l. 370. **quove.** The particle **-ve**, attached to the ends of words, means ' or '. **quo** is the adverb, ' whither '.

quaerenti agrees with **ei** (fem.) understood. **verbis** must be supplied with **talibus** and **respondit** as verb to the nominative **illi** : ' to her, questioning him in such terms, he replied '.

l. 371. **trahens vocem,** speaking with effort, that is.

l. 372. **O dea.** Aeneas is not to be deceived by the disclaimer of divinity Venus makes in ll. 335, 336. He believes her to be a goddess though he is not aware till ll. 405, 406 that she is his own divine mother.

ll. 372-374. The sentence is irregularly constructed. It opens with two 'if' clauses, with their verbs, **pergam** and **vacet,** in the present subjunctive. Such protases would normally be followed by an apodosis (main clause) with its verb in the same mood and tense, as in **si roget, respondeam,** ' if he were to ask, I should answer '. Instead the verb of the apodosis, **componet,** is future indicative. The presence of **ante** seems to show that the sentence falls between two stools, the poet having had in mind *two* modes of expression, (i) if I *were to* proceed . . . the Evening Star *would lay to rest* . . .' and (ii) ' if I *proceed* . . . the Evening Star *will lay to rest* . . . before I have done '. Vergil begins with (i) and ends with (ii).

l. 372. **repetens,** ' tracing (events) back '.

l. 373. **et (si) vacet (tibi),** ' and if there were to be leisure for thee ', i.e. ' and if thou shouldst have leisure '. **vacet** is here an impersonal verb.

ante is an adverb, 'first'—i.e. before I finish my story.

l. 374. **clauso Olympo** (abl. absolute) is an example of the principle noted at l. 69. Translate as if the Latin were **claudet Olympum et,** ' will veil the sky and . . .'

ll. 375-377. The order is **tempestas, sua forte, appulit nos, vectos per diversa aequora Troiā antiquā—si forte nomen Troiae iit per vestras aures—Libycis oris.** But the extreme flexibility of Latin word order has allowed Vergil to place the words that really matter, **Troia** and **nos**, in an emphatic position at the beginning of the sentence, and you should do the same as far as possible. Begin, ' From ancient Troy, if haply Troy's name has passed through your ears . , .'

l. 377. **forte sua,** lit., ' by its own chance ', i.e. ' at its whim '. **oris,** dative.

ll. 378, 379. **raptos,** etc. The order is **qui veho mecum classe penates raptos ex hoste.**

l. 379. **classe,** '*in* my fleet ', but instrumental, (' with . . .') in the poet's mind.

fama, abl., as scansion shows: ' by reputation '. It belongs with **notus.**

super aethera, ' above the sky ', i.e. ' in heaven '. The gods, he says, are familiar with his name. **aethera,** acc. sing., Greek form.

l. 380. Aeneas calls Italy his ' homeland ' because he is a descendant of Dardanus who came from that country and founded Troy. In a sense then, Aeneas' quest of Italy is a returning home.

The words ' a line (sprung) from Jove most high ' also allude to Dardanus, who was a son of Jove.

l. 381. **denis,** distributive numeral, is put for **decem,** cardinal, as **terna** for **tria** in l. 266. ' Twice ten ' for ' twenty ' is a familiar device to avoid the prosaic. Compare Coleridge, *Kubla Khan* :

> ' So twice five miles of fertile ground
> With walls and towers were girdled round.'

conscendi. To us it is a bold metaphor to say ' I climbed the Phrygian sea ', meaning, I put out upon it. But whereas in English we go ' down to the sea in ships ' the ancients viewed their voyaging as an ascent to ' the high seas '.

l. 382. The two phrases go better in English if reversed : ' following my allotted destiny and with my goddess-mother showing (me) the way '.

l. 383. **undis Euroque,** abl. of the instrument with **convulsae.**

l. 385. **Europa,** abl., as also **Asia.** The quantity of the final -a of **Europa** is disguised by the elision.

querentem agrees with **eum** understood. We should expect, and must translate as if we had, the infinitive **queri,** to which **eum** is subject. The words depend on **passa** : ' not suffering him to complain further '.

plura is called an adverbial accusative. It can be seen that its force is the same as that which such an adverb as **diutius** would have had.

l. 386. **medio dolore,** an ablative of time, telling *when* Venus interrupted : ' in the midst of his lamentation '.

l. 387. **haud.** Take this with **invisus. Haud invisus caelestibus** is put by litotes—artistic understatement—for ' a favourite of the gods '. **credo,** ' I believe ', is in parenthesis and has no effect on the construction of the following words.

auras vitales, ' the breath of life '.

l. 388. **qui adveneris,** 'seeing that thou hast come'. **Qui** + the subjunctive mood often = ' since '.

l. 388. **Tyriam urbem.** The preposition **ad** is often omitted in poetry. Cf. note on l. 365.

l. 389. **te ... perfer,** lit., ' convey thyself ' = ' betake thyself '.

l. 390. **namque ... nuntio ...** Order for translation : **namque nuntio tibi socios reduces classemque relatam** (esse), etc. **reduces** from **redux.**

l. 391. **tutum,** neut. of adj., used as noun, ' safety '. **versis Aquilonibus,** abl. absol. ' the north winds having been changed ' = ' when the n. winds changed '. **actam,** i.e., **actam esse.**

l. 392. **vani,** grammatically in agreement with **parentes** (*nom. pl.*), but best translated as an adverb, ' to no purpose '. **docuere = docuerunt.**

ll. 393-6. These lines describe the omen and the next three give its interpretation.

l. 393. **laetantes,** grammatically in agreement with **cycnos,** the object of **aspice,** but best rendered by adj. ' joyous ' in agreement with **agmine,** ' troop '. **senos**=**sex** (cf. l. 381 and note).

l. 394. Order for translation: **quos ales Iovis lapsa** ('swooping') **plaga aetheria** ('from the expanse of sky') **turbabat aperto caelo.**

ll. 395-396. Some editors translate as follows : ' Now in long array they seem either to choose their ground or to gaze down upon the ground they have chosen ', lit., ' the having been chosen (ground) '.

Others take **capere** to mean ' to alight on ', and **captas** to mean **captas ab aliis,** rendering as follows : ' now they are seen to alight or gaze down on the place where their comrades have alighted '. The latter is supported chiefly by the fact that the elaborate interpretation of ll. 399-401 breaks down badly if we choose the first rendering.

l. 397. **ut,** ' as '. **reduces,** ' safe-returned ', in agreement with **illi,** nom. pl. subject ' they '.

l. 398. **coetu,** ' in company '.

cantusque dedere, ' and have uttered songs '. The swans of ancient literature are birds capable of the most musical song.

l. 399. **haud aliter,** lit., ' not otherwise ' = ' even so '. These words introduce the interpretation of the omen described in the previous lines.

The twelve swans chased by an eagle are equivalent to the twelve ships of Aeneas driven by a storm. Just as some swans have alighted and others are preparing to alight, so some ships are already in the harbour, and others just entering it.

pubes tuorum, ' the youth of thy (men) ' = ' thy comrades '.

l. 400. **pleno velo,** ' with—we say ' under '—full sail.'

l. 402. **avertens,** intransitive, ' turning away ', i.e. ' as she turned away '. **rosea cervice refulsit,** lit., ' she gleamed with roseate neck '. Make ' roseate neck ' the subject. The **re-** in

refulsit might be rendered ' bright ' as it conveys the idea of something standing out clearly against a dark background.

ambrosiae comae, ' ambrosial hair '. Page in his edition has an interesting note that **ambrosia** meant either the food of the gods or an unguent of the gods, and that here the adjective ' ambrosial ' is connected with its second meaning.

l. 403. **vertice,** abl. of separation ' from her head '.

l. 405. **et vera . . . dea,** ' and by her gait she was revealed, a very goddess '.

l. 406. **tali . . . secutus,** lit., ' he pursued (her) fleeing with such a voice ' = ' he pursued her as she fled with these words '.

l. 407. **quid,** ' why '. **quid** is strictly the neuter accusative singular of **quis,** used adverbially.

l. 407. order for translation : **tu quoque crudelis, quid ludis natum totiens falsis imaginibus** '.

tu quoque crudelis, ' thou also cruel ', i.e. as well as everything else.

l. 408-409. **cur . . . non datur,** ' why is it not given to me ? ', i.e. ' why am I not allowed '.

l. 409. **veras . . . voces,** ' words unfeigned ' *or* ' undisguised '.

l. 410. **talibus.** Supply **verbis.** The object of **incusat** is **eam** understood. **tendit,** ' directs '.

l. 411. **gradientes,** ' (them) going ' = ' them, as they went ' Achates is with Aeneas : hence the plural.

l. 412. **et multo . . . amictu,** ' and enfolded them, goddess (as she was), in a thick (**multo**) mantle of cloud '.

Note : (i) **circum . . . fudit** = **circumfudit,** an example of tmesis, ' cutting ', i.e. separation of the preposition and the verb in a compound verb. (ii) **dea,** nominative in apposition with the subject, ' she '.

l. 413. **ne quis . . . neu quis,** ' that no one . . . and no one '.

l. 414. **moliri . . . poscere.** The infinitives depend on **posset** in the previous line.

l. 415. **Paphum,** ' to Paphos ', a city on the island of Cyprus, especially sacred to Venus and possessing a famous temple to her. **sublimis,** lit., ' on high ' = ' through the sky '.

l. 416. **laeta,** adj. for adverb, ' joyfully '. **illi,** dative, ' to her ' = ' in her honour '. Take this immediately after **ubi.**

l. 417. **Sabaeo ture,** ' with Sabaean incense '. The Sabaeans were a people in South-West Arabia who were closely associated with the important frankincense trade which came from the Southern Shore of Arabia (the Hadramaut) via the Red Sea trading ports on the Egyptian coast, across the desert to the Nile, thence via Alexandria to Rome and the West.

It is unlikely that Vergil knew accurately the source of frankincense which had been a trade secret for many years among the Arabs. However, Roman poets used the names of Eastern tribes and people indiscriminately to denote the East or Near East, and Vergil has luckily applied the correct adjective this time.

l. 418. **corripuere viam,** ' they have sped on the road '. The use of **corripio,** lit., ' seize ', is akin to the English expression ' take the road ', but adds the notion of swiftness.

qua, relative adverb, ' where '. **semita monstrat,** ' the pathway points '.

l. 419. **qui plurimus urbi imminet,** ' which very much looms over the city ', i.e. ' which looms large ', etc.

l. 420. **adversasque . . . arces,** ' and from above looks towards the towers opposite '.

l. 421. **molem,** ' the mass ' = ' the massive city ' : **magalia quondam,** ' once (mere) huts '. **magalia** is a Phoenician, not a Latin word, used by Vergil to give ' local colour '.

l. 422. **strata viarum,** poetic for **stratas vias,** ' paved streets '. **strata** is acc. pl. neut. of the perfect participle.

l. 423. **instant ardentes Tyrii . . . . muros,** ' the Tyrians hotly press on; some to build walls ', etc.

The infinitives **ducere, moliri, subvolvere, optare, concludere,** are all dependent on **instant,** which in this passage contains the idea of ' desire '.

Note that the subject **Tyrii** is split up into two nominatives, **pars ... pars,** ' some ... others '. The noun **pars** is often put for **alii.**

l. 426. **iura ... senatum,** ' laws and magistrates (accusative) they choose, and a reverend senate '.

Commentators note that Vergil, had he lived long enough, would probably have struck out this line, partly because, interrupting as it does the description of the building, it seems out of place, partly because Vergil is applying Roman customs and institutions of a much later stage in the evolution of a democracy to the actual building of a town in a period when kings were supreme rulers of their states.

l. 427. **hic,** adverb. **portus,** acc. pl.

l. 429. **rupibus,** ' from the cliffs '. **scaenis ... futuris,** ' lofty adornments for the stage to be '.

l. 430-431. **qualis ... labor,** lit., ' (such is) [1] the labour as **(qualis)** makes the bees busy in the early summer amid the flowery countryside in the sunshine ' ; e.g. ' even as the bees are kept busy with the labour ', etc.

For this simile, compare Vergil's *Georgics*, IV, ll. 162-169 and remember that it would come easily to the mind of a man who had spent his youth in the country, on a farm.

l. 431. **cum,** ' when '.

adultos fetus, ' the full-grown young ', object of **educunt.**

l. 434. **onera venientum,** ' the burdens of (bees) coming '. object of **accipiunt,** i.e. ' the burdens of incomers '. **venientum** put for the usual **venientium.**

agmine facto, abl. abs., ' forming an army '.

l. 435. Order for translation : **arcent fucos, ignavum pecus, a praesepibus.**

---

[1] **Talis est** to be supplied.

l. 436. **fervet opus,** ' the work is aglow '. The wurd **ferveo,** ' seethe ', conjures in the mind of the observant the ceaseless and seemingly random activity at the hive's mouth.

l. 437. **O fortunati,** supply **sunt,** ' fortunate are they '. Aeneas, after seven years' wandering over the Mediterranean Sea in an unsuccessful search for the site of the new town which it was his destiny to establish, naturally envies those who have just settled in Carthage, and are now busily engaged in the exciting task of building the city.

l. 439. **infert se ; se inferre** is often used in the meaning of ' to betake oneself ', ' to go into ', ' to enter '.

mirabile dictu, ' wonderful in the telling ', i.e. ' to tell '. **dictu** is the ablative of the supine, which is a verbal noun. The ablative is one of respect. This use of the supine is found chiefly after adjectives.

l. 440. **per medios,** supply **viros.** Supply **se** (from the previous line) with **miscet,** ' and mixes with the men '.

neque cernitur ulli, ' and is not seen by anyone '. Note **ulli,** dative of the agent, found in poetry with most tenses of the passive, but more commonly with the perfect.

Some take this use as a dative of the person interested, ' is not visible to anyone '.

l. 441. **laetissimus umbrae,** ' most rich in shade '. Note the genitive, used after adjectives denoting ' want ' or ' fullness '. Cf. ll. 14 and 343.

l. 442. **quo ... signum ;** order for translation : **locus quo** (' in which ') **primum Poeni, iactati undis et turbine, effodere** (= **effoderunt) signum.**

In the text **locus** is attracted into the case of the relative pronoun.

l. 444. **monstrarat = monstraverat. caput acris equi,** ' a head of a spirited horse '.

A horse's head was the symbol of Carthage and so often found on Carthaginian coins. The horse is also a symbol of war and wealth and hence the significance of **sic** in the same line.

sic nam fore ... gentem, ' for thus (she said) the race
would be outstanding in war and rich in food through the ages'.
fore, fut. infin. of **sum** in acc. and infin. construction dependent
on a verb of saying which can easily be supplied from the
verb **monstrarat.**

l. 446. **hic,** adverb.   **ingens,** acc. sg. neut. in agreement with
templum.

l. 447. **donis ... divae,** ' rich (**opulentum** in agreement with
templum) in gifts and the presence of the goddess '.

l. 448. **aerea cui ... aenis,** lit., ' to which the bronze threshold
rose on steps, the beams (were) bound with bronze, the hinge
creaked on the doors of bronze '.

Note (i) that the emphasis falls on the three words **aerea,
aere, aenis.**   (ii) **limina** = the whole doorway ; **fores,** the
actual doors.   (iii) **nexae aere,** ' bound with bronze ', i.e. not
with bronze rivets, but consisting of bronze plates riveted
together.   (iv) **cui** = **cuius** = ' its '.   Latin often has dative
where English has the genitive.   (v) **nexaeque** : the vowel of
the hypermetric syllable **que** is elided before the first syllable
of the next line.

Translate : ' bronze were the portals that rose on steps,
of bronze the bolted frames, and on bronze doors the hinges
creaked.'

l. 450. **nova res oblata,** ' a strange thing offered ' = ' the
appearance of a strange thing ', subject of **leniit.**

l. 452. **ausus,** supply **est.**

rebus adflictis depends on **confidere,** which takes the dative
The words may be translated ' his shattered fortunes '.

ll. 453-455. Order for translation : **namque dum sub ingenti
templo lustrat singula** (neut. pl. = ' each object '), **opperiens
reginam, dum miratur quae sit fortuna urbi** (= urbis)
manusque artificum inter se laboremque operum

l. 455. ' the craftsmanship of the several artists and the
labour of their tasks '. **inter se,** ' amongst themselves ', i.e. ' as
compared with one another '.

l. 457. ' and the wars now published by report throughout the whole world '.

l. 458. **Atridas,** ' the sons of Atreus ', i.e. Agamemnon and Menelaus, the leaders of the Greeks in the Trojan war.

Achillem saevum ambobus, ' Achilles fierce against both ' i.e. against both the Atridae and Priam.

During the Trojan war Achilles quarrelled with Agamemnon over a captive girl and remained ' sulking ' in his tent until, roused by the death of his closest friend Patroclus, he resumed the battle and finally slew Hector, the great champion of the Trojans and son of the aged king of Troy, Priam.

l. 459. **lacrimans.** The Romans and Greeks were not ashamed of tears, in strong contrast to the practice of modern Englishmen. As Page, however, in his edition notes, it is feeble to refer three times to the tears of Aeneas as he gazes at these pictures.

Achate, vocative of **Achates.**

l. 460. Supply **est** as the verb to this sentence.

l. 461. **Sunt . . . ,** ' there are here also its own rewards to fame ' ; i.e. ' here also fame has its own rewards '.

l. 462. **sunt . . . tangunt,** a very beautiful and famous line which is almost untranslatable. Lit., ' there are tears for things and mortal (life) touches the heart '. **Res** is almost ' troubles ' and **mortalia,** ' mortal things ', means ' the sorrows of mankind '.

l. 463. **metus,** acc. pl., **aliquam salutem,** ' some help '. aliquis is pathetic : men can expect only imperfect happiness.

l. 464. **pictura inani,** ' on the unsubstantial picture ', an awkward expression in English. Vergil calls the picture ' unsubstantial ' because it is only a representation of the comrades whom Aeneas has lost and now mourns.

l. 465. **multa gemens,** ' groaning deeply '. **multa,** acc. neut. pl. Neuter pronouns and adjectives are often used in the accusative to modify a verb *from within* (internal or adverbial accusative).

flumine, tears, of course.

l. 466. **uti = ut,** 'how' introducing indirect questions : hence the subjunctives, **fugerent, premeret, instaret.**

bellantes circum Pergama. This participial phrase qualifies all the nominatives in ll. 466-467.

l. 468. **hac Phryges.** Supply **fugerent** as the verb and introduce 'while' before **cristatus Achilles curru instaret.**

Thus the pictures in these three lines represent the Greeks in flight with the Trojans in pursuit, then the Trojans in flight with the Greeks in pursuit.

ll. 469-493. The pictures which are described in these lines are also in pairs. (i) The death of Rhesus, followed by the death of Troilus. (2) The Trojan women as suppliants of Pallas, followed by Priam supplicating Achilles. (3) Aeneas himself and Memnon, followed by the fighting of the Amazons under their queen, Penthesilea.

Incidents from the Trojan War and other epic stories were frequently portrayed in pictures, sculptures, and friezes in the houses and temples of the ancient world.

l. 469 **niveis tentoria velis,** 'tents with snowy canvas', object of **agnoscit,** l. 470.

Rhesus was a Thracian prince who came, though somewhat late on in the war, to Troy to help the Trojans, in accordance with an oracle that declared that Troy would never be captured, once his famous snow-white horses had a taste of the grass or water of Troy. On the first night of his arrival, Odysseus (or Ulysses) and Diomede (Tydides, 471) entered as spies into the Trojan camp which was, at that stage in the Trojan war, pitched outside the walls of the city on the plain of Troy, and succeeded in murdering Rhesus and capturing his famous horses.

This incident forms the subject of a Greek play 'Rhesus', attributed to Euripides, a drama which inspired Drinkwater's one-act play, '$x = o$'.

ll. 470-471. Order for translation : **quae, prodita primo somno, cruentus Tydides vastabat multa caede.**

prodita . . . somno, ' betrayed by the first sleep '. The first sleep is the deepest and therefore most likely to betray them, i.e. expose them to sudden death at the hands of an assassin.

Tydides, a patronymic, ' the son of Tydeus ' = ' Diomede '.

l. 472. **ardentes,** ' fiery ', in agreement with **equos.**

l. 473. ' before they could taste . . . and could drink '. The subjunctives **gustassent** (= **gustavissent**), **bibissent,** express in the oblique form the *fut. perfect* of direct speech.

Xanthum. The Xanthus was a river near Troy.

l. 474. **parte alia,** ' on another side ', i.e. elsewhere in the temple, whose mural paintings Aeneas is studying. Troilus was the youngest son of Priam, slain by Achilles.

l. 475. **infelix . . . Achilli,** ' unhappy boy and unequally matched (in combat) with Achilles ', lit., ' having met Achilles unequal '.

l. 476. **fertur . . . inani,** ' is carried (along) by his horses, and fallen backward (**resupinus**) (still) clings to the empty car '.

l. 477. **huic cervix,** '*his* neck'. Note the dative of the pronoun where we use the possessive adjective.

l. 478. **et versa . . . hasta,** ' and the dust is scored by his turned (i.e. reversed) spear '.

l. 479. **non aequae,** ' not kind ' = ' cruel ', in agreement with **Palladis.**

l. 480. **Iliades,** ' the Trojan women ', subject of **ibant,** l. 479.

passis, from **pando.**

peplum. The robe was properly a long white one, offered to Pallas Athene every five years at Athens during her great festival the Panathenaea. The procession is portrayed on the friezes of the Parthenon. They can be seen in the Elgin room at the British Museum.

l. 481. **tunsae pectora,** 'beating their breasts'. For the perfect participle passive used in a middle sense with a direct object, see the note on l. 228.

Note also the *present* meaning of this *perfect* participle, a use which is fairly frequent in the case of deponent verbs and probably arose from the absence of a present participle passive in Latin.

l. 482. ' The goddess, turned away, kept her eyes fixed on the ground'. **aversa,** 'turned away', i.e. 'with averted face'. This describes Athena's implacable hostility to the Trojan cause.

Note **sŏlo,** 'on the ground'. **Sōlum,** 'soil', 'ground' but **sōlus,** 'alone'.

l. 483. **Hectora,** accusative.   -a is the accusative ending ot the Greek third declension.

ll. 483-484. It is obvious that the painter could not represent Achilles dragging Hector's body three times round the walls of Troy.

Perhaps the use of the pluperfect **raptaverat** and then of the imperfect **vendebat** suggests that Aeneas has added the first line as an introduction to the subject of the picture which is the sale of the corpse, no doubt represented as grievously mangled.

The single combat between Achilles and Hector occurs in Book XXII of the *Iliad*. The beginning of Book XXIV describes how in revenge for the murder of his friend Patroclus, Achilles drags Hector's body thrice round his tomb. The same book tells how the aged Priam set forth from Troy to the Greek camp to ransom his son's corpse. These two books are well worth reading in translation.

l. 485. **dat** = ' utters ' and its subject is ' he ', standing for Aeneas.

l. 486. **ut,** ' as '. In the meaning ' as ' or ' when ', ut is regularly followed by the indicative.

l. 488. **se quoque . . . Achivis,** ' he recognised himself also mingling (in combat) with the Greek chieftains '. **permixtum** is literally passive, ' mingled ', and **principibus** probably dative, a case common in a variety of meanings after verbs compounded with prepositions.

It is interesting to notice that in the *Iliad* Aeneas is only a secondary character.

l. 489. **Eoasque ... arma.** Memnon, the king of the Aethiopians, assisted Priam towards the end of the Trojan war. He was slain by Achilles. He was the son of Dawn (Aurora or Eos) ; hence **Eoasque acies.** See also l. 751.

l. 490. **lunatis agmina peltis,** ' columns with crescent shields ', object of **ducit,** with **Penthesilea furens** as subject. The ablative is similar to the ablative of description or quality, which always consists of noun + adjective.

l. 491. **Penthesilea furens,** ' Penthesilea in fury '. After the death of Hector, Penthesilea, queen of the Amazons, brought her female warriors to aid Priam and Troy. She was eventually slain by Achilles. The fighting of Greeks and Amazons was a favourite subject in Greek art and sculpture.

The Amazons are a mythical race who were said to originate from the Caucasus region. Their name, which in Greek means ' breastless ', led the story-tellers to explain that they removed their right breasts to facilitate the use of the bow.

l. 492. **aurea ... mammae,** ' binding a golden girdle neath (one) breast displayed ' (= ' neath one naked breast'). **exsertae mammae** is dative, a case commonly found after compound verbs. ,

l. 493. **bellatrix ... ,** ' a warrior-queen, and dares, (though) a maid, to engage in battle with men '.

viris, dat. in association with the compound verb **concurrere.**

l. 494. **haec dum ... videntur,** ' while these wonders are being seen by Dardanian Aeneas.

Note : (i) **Aeneae,** dative of the agent. Cf. the note on l. 440. (ii) **Dardanio Aeneae** : there is no hiatus here, for the vowel o of **Dardanio** is elided before **Aeneae.** (iii) **Dardanio.** Dardanus was an ancestor of the Trojans : hence = ' Trojan.'

Cf. Teucri, also meaning 'Trojans' from Teucer, another legendary king of Troy.

l. 495. **obtutuque** . . . **in uno,** 'and sticks fixed in one gaze ', i.e. ' and stands fast, gazing raptly '.

l. 496. **forma,** abl. of respect with **pulcherrima,** nom., in agreement with **Dido** : ' Dido, most fair of form '.

l. 497. **incessit,** ' stept forth '. Vergil often uses this verb of goddesses and queens. See also l. 46.

magna . . . **caterva,** ablative absolute, ' a great throng pressing (her close) '.

l. 498. **qualis,** render here by ' even as '. **Eurotae,** gen. of **Eurotas,** a river in Laconia (southern part of Greece) ; **Cynthus,** a mountain in the island of Delos. Both places were favourite haunts of Diana.

l. 499. **quam** . . . **Oreades,** ' having followed whom a thousand mountain nymphs assemble from here and from there ' ; i.e. ' in whose train a thousand mountain nymphs troop on either side '.

l. 501. **gradiens,** ' going ', i.e. ' as she goes '.

l. 502. **Latonae** . . . **pectus. gaudia,** neut. pl., ' joy ', is the subject. **tacitum,** ' secret ' in agreement with **pectus.** Latona is the mother of Diana : hence her joy as she contemplates her daughter's beauty.

l. 503. **talem** . . . **ferebat,** ' such she bore herself joyful ' = ' so she moved joyfully '.

l. 504. **instans** . . . **futuris,** ' urging on the work and her future empire ' = ' the work of her future empire '.

Note the hendiadys—a literary device which is very common in Latin poetry, but rare in English. The essence of it is that two nouns, one of which should be grammatically dependent on the other, are put in the same case and connected by ' **et** '.

l. 505. **tum** . . . **resedit,** ' then at the doors of the goddess, beneath the central dome of the temple, encircled with arms and resting on a throne on high, she took her seat '.

armis is put for **armatis**.

foribus divae. These doors give entrance, not to the temple proper, but to the interior shrine at the back of the main portion of the temple. This shrine has a domed or vaulted roof. Vergil makes Dido hold her session in a temple, very much as the Roman senate used to hold its meetings in various temples.

l. 507. **viris,** ' to her people '.

ll. 507-508. **operumque . . . trahebat,** ' and she made equal their laborious tasks (lit., the labour of their tasks) by fair division or apportioned them by lot '.

l. 509. **cum,** ' when '.

l. 510. **Anthea,** acc. of **Antheus :** see note on l. 483. **Anthea** and the following accusatives are subjects of **concedere** (l. 509) in the *acc.* and *infin.* construction, dependent on **videt.**

ll. 511-512. **ater quos . . . oras,** ' whom the black storm had scattered over the sea and had carried far away to other shores '.

l. 513. **simul . . . simul :** often is equivalent to ' both . . . and '.

ipse = Aeneas. **Achates** is also nom. to **obstipuit,** and **percussus,** though singular, goes in sense with both.

l. 514. **avidi,** ' eagerly ' ; adj. for adverb as often.

l. 515. **coniungere ardebant,** ' they burned to clasp '. The infinitive after **ardeo** is poetical, but understandable from the use here of **ardeo** in the sense ' am eager '.

res incognita, lit., ' thing unknown ' = ' their ignorance of the situation '.

l. 516. **dissimulant,** ' they conceal (their desire) '.

l. 517. **quae fortuna viris.** Supply **sit,** the whole clause being an indirect question, dependent on **speculantur,** ' watch to see '. ' What fortune there is to the men ' = ' What fortune the men meet with '.

quo litore, ' (on) what shore '.

l. 518. **quid,** ' why '.   **cunctis navibus,** ' from all the ships '.

l. 520. **introgressi,** supply **sunt,** and **est** with **data.**

coram, adv., ' in the presence (of the queen) '.

l. 521. **maximus,** ' the eldest '.   In prose **maximus natu** is regularly used as the superlative of **senex.**

placido pectore, ' with unruffled bosom '.   Ilioneus shows no sign of fear.

ll. 522-523. **cui condere Iuppiter . . dedit,** ' to whom Jupiter has given to found '.   **condere** is the infinitive used as a verbal noun, here in the accusative case as the object of the verb **dedit. frenare** is in the same construction.

l. 524. **ventis . . . vecti,** ' borne by the winds (over) every sea '.

l. 525. **prohibe,** etc.   Ilioneus fears that the natives may burn the Trojan fleet.

l. 526. **propius . . . nostras,** ' look more kindly on our fortunes ', lit., ' more nearly '.

l. 527. **penates,** lit., ' guardian deities of the household ', is often used to denote ' home ', as here.

ll. 527-528. **populare venimus . . . vertere.** Note the infinitive expressing purpose—only rarely found and then after verbs of motion.   In prose we should have **ut** + subjunctive.

l. 528. **raptas . . . praedas,** ' stolen booty '.   **vertere,** ' drive ', for the natural booty would be cattle.

l. 529. **ea,** ' such '.   Supply **est** as the verb.

animo and **victis** are datives.

l. 530. **est,** ' (there) is '.   **Hesperiam,** ' Western Land ' is often used by the Roman poets of Italy.

dicunt, ' call (it) '.

l. 531. **armis** and **ubere** are ablatives of respect, ' in arms ', etc.

l. 532. **Oenotri,** ' the Oenotrians '—an old Italian race who had originally settled in south Italy.   The name of their district Oenotria seems to mean 'Wine-land'. **coluere** = **coluerunt**.

l. 533. **nunc fama . . .** , 'now (there is) a report that the younger (folk) have called the race Italian from their leader's name'. **minores,** supply **natu,** 'younger'. **ducis:** Italus is meant, a mythical hero, from whom, as we learn here, the country is said to have taken its name.

l. 534. **hic cursus fuit.** 'This (i.e. hither) was our course'. This is the first of fifty-five unfinished lines in the Aeneid—a sign that Vergil had been unable to complete the revision of his great work.

ll. 535. **cum,** 'when'. **subito,** adjective in agreement with **fluctu.**

adsurgens nimbosus Orion, 'stormy Orion, rising'.

The constellation Orion set in the month of November and so was considered by the ancients to usher in the period of stormy weather which was prevalent at that time. The storm described in these lines, however, occurred in summer when Orion was beginning to rise. But there is no need to expect Vergil to be exact in such matters.

ll. 536-538. **penitusque . . . dispulit,** 'and with boisterous south winds scattered us far (**penitus**) amid the waves, the surge overwhelming (us), and amid pathless rocks'. **superante salo** is an abl. absol. Perhaps we might render, 'amid the waves with their overwhelming surge'. **invia** must suggest that the rocks among which they find themselves are uninhabited islands, or, more probably, that there is no safe channel between them.

l. 538. **pauci,** 'we few'.

l. 539. Supply **est** after **quod.**

ll. 539-540. **quaeve . . . patria,** 'or what land (is) so barbarous (that it) permits this custom'. The next lines explain what the custom is.

l. 540. **hospitio . . . harenae,** 'we are debarred from the welcome of the beach'.

l. 541. **cient, vetant** : the subject, 'they', is the inhabitants of the land. **prima . . . terra,** ablative as often in poetry without the preposition **in,** 'on the edge (or border) of their land '.

l. 543. **at sperate . . . nefandi,** ' yet expect gods, mindful of right and wrong ' = ' look for gods who do not forget right and wrong '. Note that **spero** does not always mean ' hope '.

l. 544. **nobis,** dative, should be translated as if you had **noster. quo iustior . . .** lit., ' than whom (abl. of comparison) another was neither more righteous in piety nor . . .' = ' than whom no other was more righteous . . .'.

l. 546. **quem,** ' which ' = ' that ', qualifying **virum,** i.e. Aeneas. **vescitur,** meaning here ' breathes ', is followed by the ablative, **aura aetheria,** ' air of heaven '.

crudelibus . . . umbris, ' in the cruel shades ', i.e. in the Underworld.

l. 547. **non metus.** Supply **est.** ' Fear is not ' means ' we have no fear '.

ll. 547-548. **officio . . . paeniteat,** ' nor would it repent thee to have striven the first in kindness ', i.e. ' nor wouldst thou repent to have been the first to strive in (showing) kindness '.

l. 549. **Siculis regionibus.** Supply **in. et,** ' also '. The thought is that even if Aeneas is dead, in Sicily they have a friend who will give them a settlement to live in and will recompense Dido for her kindness.

l. 550. **arma,** ' strength '. One MS. has **arva,** which is perhaps preferable as concealing no threat.

a sanguine : render **a** by ' of '.

l. 551. **liceat subducere,** lit., ' let it be allowed (us) to beach ', i.e. ' allow us to beach '. **liceat,** jussive subjunctive, expressing a command in the 3rd person.

l. 552. **silvis.** Supply **in. stringere remos,** ' to strip oars ', i.e. ' to trim boughs into oars '. For a simple example of this use (called ' proleptic ') of the noun, compare ' to mix a drink ', which really means ' mix ingredients into a drink '.

ll. 553-554. Order for translation: **ut,** (l. 554 'in order that') **si datur** ('it is granted') **tendere Italiam, recepto sociis et rege, laeti** ('joyfully') **petamus Italiam. Latiumque tendere Italiam,** 'to make for Italy'. **recepto** should be **receptis,** agreeing with both **sociis** and **rege** in the ablative absolute.

l. 555. **absumpta.** Supply **est. Teucrum,** genitive plural.

l. 556. **nec spes . . . Iuli,** 'and no hope remains now in Julus'.

ll. 557-558. Order for translation : **ut** (supplied from l. 554) **at** ('at any rate') **petamus freta Sicaniae . . .**

l. 558. **unde huc advecti.** Supply **sumus ;** 'whence we sailed hither'.

regem, '(as) king', in apposition with **Acesten.**

l. 559. **Ilioneus.** Supply 'spoke' as the verb, and **verbis** with **talibus. ore fremebant,** 'shouted assent,' lit., 'made a noise with the mouth'.

l. 561. **vultum demissa,** lit., 'downcast as to her face', **vultum** being an accusative of respect ; i.e. 'with downcast face'. The prose construction would be **vultu demisso.**

It is also possible to explain it as an accusative, object of the perfect participle passive used in a middle sense, i.e. 'having dropped her eyes. '.

l. 562. Vergil might more logically have written, and we must translate, **solvite corda metu,** 'free your hearts from fear', but the poet typically prefers the variation 'free fear from your hearts'.

l. 563. **res dura,** 'hard thing' = 'hard fortune '.

l. 564. **me talia cogunt moliri,** 'compel me to do such deeds ', such as watching the coast carefully.

custode, singular for plural, 'with guards '.

l. 565. **quis . . . nesciat,** 'who could be ignorant of the race of Aeneas' people . . .' Potential subjunctive.

l. 566. **virtutes,** abstract for concrete, 'brave deeds'

incendia, ' flames ', used metaphorically, war being compared to a conflagration.

ll. 567-568. **non obtunsa . . . ab urbe,** 'we Carthaginians do not bear such unfeeling hearts nor does the Sun yoke his steeds so far (**aversus**) from (our) Tyrian town '. **Adeo** merely emphasises **obtunsa.** Dido means that she and her people are not such boors nor so far distant from civilisation as not to have heard of the Trojans. The ancient world of Greece and Rome regarded the Mediterranean basin and the surrounding lands as the centre of the known and civilised world, over which the sun moved in his course by day.

l. 569. **Saturnia arva.** Saturn was a mythical king of Italy whom the Romans regarded as the father of Jupiter. His name is connected with the verb **sero, -ere, sevi, satum,** ' I sow ', and he was said to have introduced agriculture and the arts of civilisation, and to have inaugurated a golden age of peace and plenty. Here ' the fields of Saturn ' = Italy.

l. 570. **Erycis fines,** ' the territories of Eryx ', i.e. Sicily, Eryx being the name of a mountain in that island. **regem,** in apposition with Acesten, ' as king '.

l. 571. **tutos,** agrees with **vos** (understood) and is the object of **dimittam** ; lit., ' safe with help ' = ' protected by an escort '.

l. 572. **et,** ' also '. Dido here offers the Trojans a third choice, a share in her own colony. **his regnis,** i.e. **in his regnis.**

l. 573. **urbem quam . . . est.** Note that **urbem** is attracted into the case of its relative pronoun. Translate as if **urbs** were the reading.

l. 574. **mihi,** ' by me ', or ' in my eyes '. For the dative, see the note on l. 440.

ll. 575-576. ' Oh that (your) king himself, even Aeneas, were here, driven by the same South wind '. **adforet = adesset.** This subjunctive, which expresses a wish for the present, is called ' optative '.

l. 576. **certos,** ' trusty men '.

l. 577. **extrema**, acc. pl. neut. of the adjective used as a noun : ' furthermost parts '.

l. 578. ' in case (**si**) perchance he is wandering in any woods or town, a shipwrecked man ' (**eiectus**). **quibus** from the indefinite adjective **qui, quae, quod**, ' any ', used after **si, nisi, num, ne**.

l. 579. **animum**, ' in spirit ', accusative of respect with **arrecti**, which is nom. masc. plural to agree with **Achates et Aeneas**. The **et** before **fortis** means ' both '.

l. 580. **erumpere nubem**, ' to break through the cloud '. **Erumpere** has its literal and transitive meaning of ' sunder ' ; its commonest use, however, is intransitive, ' burst forth *or* from '. For the infinitive with **ardeo**, cf. l. 515.

l. 582. **nate dea**, ' o thou born of a goddess '. **dea**, ablative of origin, a development of the ablative of separation. **animo**, ' local ' ablative.

l. 584. **unus abest**, i.e. Orontes ; see ll. 113-117.

l. 585. **dictis**, etc. The promises of Venus are true in all else.

l. 586. **circumfusa**, ' enveloping ', with **nubes**.

l. 587. **scindit se ... purgat**, ' parts and clears ', lit., ' cleaves itself and clears (itself) '. The Latin reflexive verb is often equivalent to our English transitive verbs when used, as they often are, intransitively.

l. 588. **restitit ... refulsit**, ' stood forth ... and gleamed '. For the meaning of **re-** in these compounds, see the note on l. 402.

l. 589. **os ... similis**, ' like to a god in face and shoulders '. **os, umeros**, accusatives of respect.

ll. 589-591. Order for translation : **namque genetrix ipsa adflarat nato decoram caesariem purpureumque lumen iuventae et laetos honores oculis.**

decoram caesariem, ' beautiful flowing locks ' = ' the beauty of flowing locks '. **adflarat = adflaverat.**

ll. 592-593. **quale . . . auro,** ' (such) beauty as the (artist's) hands impart to ivory or when silver or Parian marble is encircled with yellow gold '.

Note : **manus,** nominative plural : **decus,** accusative singular of a neuter noun.

Paros is an island in the Aegean sea, famous for the marble quarries there.

The point of the comparisons seems to be that Venus sheds a new beauty round her hero son, in the same way as the craftsman enhances ivory, silver, or stone by a beautiful setting.

l. 594, 595. **cunctis . . . improvisus,** 'previously invisible to all '.

ll. 595-596. **coram . . . Aeneas,** ' (I), whom you seek, am present before you (**coram**), Trojan Aeneas '.

l. 597. **o sola . . . miserata,** ' o thou that alone hast pitied '. **miserata** is voc. sg. fem. of the perfect partic. : ' having pitied '.

ll. 598-600. **quae . . . socias,** ' (thou) who dost associate us . . . , in thy city, thy home ', i.e. ' thou who dost share thy city, thy home with us '.

Note that in agreement with **nos** are two phrases. **reliquias Danaum, omnium egenos.**

reliquias Danaum. See the note on l. 30.

l. 599. **omnium** is neut. pl., ' all things '.

l. 600. **grates persolvere dignas,** ' to pay fitting thanks ', is the subject of **est** in l. 601.

ll. 601-602. **non opis est . . . per orbem,** ' is not of (i.e. within) our power, nor (in the power of) whatever anywhere there is of the Trojan race that (is) scattered throughout the wide world '.

Note **quidquid est,** ' whatever there is ', + a genitive frequently means ' all there is ' of something. So here, we might say ' (in the power of) all that survive anywhere of the Trojan race . . .'.

ll. 603-605. **di tibi . . . praemia digna ferant. qua,** ' any ', is in agreement with **numina,** the subject of **respectant.**

si quid . . . est, ' if justice is aught (=has any influence) anywhere '.

ferant, present subjunctive, expressing a wish for 'the future, has two subjects, **di** (l. 603) and **mens sibi conscia recti** (l. 604), lit., ' mind conscious to itself of right ' = ' the consciousness of right '. 'May the gods . . . and the consciousness of right bring to thee fitting rewards.'

l. 605. **quae tam laeta,** ' what so happy ' = ' what happy '.

l. 606. **qui tanti,** ' what so great ' = ' what famous '. **talem,** (thee) such ' = ' so noble a child as thee. ' **genuere,** from **gigno.**

l. 607. **montibus,** ' on the mountains ', ablative of place where without **in. umbrae,** nom. pl.

l. 608. **polus dum . . . pascet,** ' while the heaven feeds the stars '. Vergil seems to be thinking of the heaven as the pasturing ground of the stars. Observe that **pascet,** like the two preceding futures, must be idiomatically rendered by the English present.

l. 609. **tuum** belongs with all three nominatives, though agreeing with **nomen** only.

l. 610. **quae . . . cumque = quaecumque :** an instance of tmesis, or ' cutting ', i.e. separation of a compound word into its separate parts.

l. 611. **petit dextra laevaque,** ' he makes for Ilioneus with his right hand, and Serestus with his left ', i.e. ' he grasps I. with his right hand, and S. with his left . . .'

l. 612. **post,** adverb, ' afterwards '.

l. 614. **viri,** genitive, depends on **aspectu** in the previous line as well as on **casu.** Dido is amazed first at the sight of the hero (i.e. at his grace and beauty) and then at his misfortunes. **primo** is an adverb.

tanto, ' so great ' = ' terrible '.

l. 615. **quis . . . casus,** ' what fate '. **nate dea.** See the note on l. 582.

l. 616. **immanibus . . . oris,** dative denoting place whither, as often in poetry, ' to these cruel shores '. Dido is thinking of the dangerous nature of the coast and the uncivilised character of the natives amongst whom she, a stranger herself, is building her new city.

l. 617. **tune = tu + ne,** the interrogative particle. Supply **es,** ' art thou that Aeneas . . .' Note that this line contains a hiatus and a spondee in the fifth foot instead of the customary dactyl—a licence which Vergil permits himself only in lines with proper names. The hiatus is between Dardanio and Anchisae, the **-o** not being elided.

l. 618. **ad undam,** ' by the wave '.

l. 619. **Teucrum.** This Teucer was a Greek, son of Telamon, king of the Greek island of Salamis opposite the mainland of Athens. On his return from Troy, he was rejected and driven away by his father, but with the aid of Belus, king of Sidon and father of Dido, he founded a new Salamis in Cyprus. Telamon refused to acknowledge his son Teucer because he had not avenged his brother Ajax, who had committed suicide in his bitter disappointment at not being awarded the arms of Achilles after the latter's death.

l. 619. **Sidona,** Greek accusative, ' to Sidon '.

Teucrum memini venire, ' I remember that Teucer came '.

l. 620. **finibus,** abl. of separation, ' from . . . '.

l. 622. **victor dicione,** lit., ' victorious beneath his sway ' = ' beneath his victorious sway '.

l. 623. **casus,** ' fate ' ; **cognitus,** supply **est iam** is superfluous, unless we care to say ' from that time *on* '.

l. 624. **Pelasgi,** ' Greek '. Pelasgi—a term, strictly applicable only to the prehistoric natives of Greece and the Mediterranean lands generally, was often used by the Roman poets of the Greek-speaking peoples of historic times. The Greek kings are the brothers, Agamemnon and Menelaus, kings of Mycenae and Sparta respectively, who led the Greek expedition against Troy.

l. 625. **hostis**, nom. **Teucer** is meant. **Teucros**, ' Trojans ', lit., ' descendants of Teucer ', legendary first king of Troy, not to be confused with the Greek Teucer above in l. 619, although he too, as his name implies, was a grandson of a king of Troy.

ferebat, lit., ' told of ' = ' extolled '.

l. 626. **seque . . . volebat**, ' and would have it that he was sprung from the ancient stock of the Teucri '. The literal meaning, ' wanted himself sprung ', is inappropriate, as it would imply that Teucer wanted to be what in fact he was.

l. 627. **agite**. The imperative of **ago** is often used to precede a second imperative and means, ' come '.

ll. 628-629. **me . . . terra**, lit., ' me too driven (**iactatam**) through many difficulties, a like fortune has willed to find rest at last in this land '.

l. 630. I.e. Dido's experience of trouble teaches her a practical sympathy with the unfortunate.

ll. 631-632. **simul . . . simul**, ' at once . . . at once '. Unlike the use in l. 513, **simul** here indicates the coincidence of her words and actions.

l. 632. **honorem**, ' sacrifice ', as in l. 49. **templis** = **in templis**

l. 633. **nec minus** here = ' also '. **sociis**, ' for his comrades '.

ll. 634, 635. **magnorum . . . suum**. Meaning to say ' a hundred great boars with bristling backs ', Vergil characteristically invents the variation ' the bristling backs of a hundred great boars '.

l. 636. **munera laetitiamque dii**, ' (as) gifts and the gladness of the day ' = ' as gifts to gladden the day '. **Dii** is an old form of **diei**.

There is a reading **dei**, i.e. gen. of **deus**, in which case ' the gladness of the god ' refers to wine.

l. 637. **regali splendida luxu,** ' splendid with princely luxury ' = ' with the splendour of princely luxury '.

ll. 639-642. **arte** . . . **gentis,** ' (there are) coverlets of proud purple embroidered with skill, massive silver (= silver plate) on the tables, and embossed in gold the brave feats of their sires, a long line of exploits (**rerum**), traced (**ducta**) through countless (**tot**) heroes from the ancient rise of the race'. In translation we must drop the **-que** which (to our minds unnaturally) joins **arte** and **ostro.**

Drinking-vessels of silver and gold were frequently embossed with scenes from legendary or historical events.

ll. 643-644. **neque enim** . . . **amor. patrius amor,** ' a father's love ', i.e. the love Aeneas feels as a father for his son Ascanius. **passus,** supply **est. consistere,** ' to rest '.

l. 644. **rapidum,** adj. for adv., ' swiftly '.

l. 645. **ferat haec,** supply **ut,** ' to bear these tidings to A '. **ducat** is likewise final subjunctive.

l. 646. **omnis** . . . **parentis,** ' in Ascanius all his loving father's care is centred '.

l. 648. The object of **iubet** is **eum** understood (= **Achaten**). **pallam** . . . **rigentem,** ' a robe stiff with figures and with gold ' = ' with figures wrought in gold '. Embroidery with gold thread was frequently used in the ancient world.

l. 649. **acantho.** Vergil means that the veil had a border on which the design was imitated from the plant acanthus with its leaf resembling a bear's paw.

l. 650. **ornatus,** acc. pl. in apposition with **pallam** and **velamen,** ' a dress of Argive Helen '. ' Argive ' here means merely ' Greek '. Helen was the wife of Menelaus, king of Sparta, and daughter of Leda.

Mycenis, ' from Mycenae ', to be taken with **extulerat,** l. 652. Mycenae was actually the town of Agamemnon, brother of Menelaus. The Roman poets did not bother too much about geographical accuracy. Mycenae and Sparta were both in the south of Greece, the former ruled over by Agamemnon, the latter by his brother Menelaus. So to Vergil, Mycenae and Sparta were almost interchangeable terms, to be used according to the demands of the metre.

l. 651. **peteret.** The final syllable, though short in quantity, is lengthened by ictus or the stress, and thus scanned as a long syllable.

inconcessos hymenaeos : ' the illicit marriage ' sought by Helen was with Paris.

l. 653. **Ilione . . . maxima natarum Priami,** ' Ilione, eldest of the daughters of Priam '. She was married to Polydorus, king of Thrace.

l. 654. **colloque . . . coronam,** ' and for the neck a circlet beaded (i.e. hung with pearls) and a coronet double with jewels and gold (i.e. a double coronet of jewels and gold) '.

l. 656. In this line **iter tendere** forms a phrase, ' to make one's way '. In l. 554 **tendere** is used alone in the same sense.

l. 657. **Cytherea.** See the note on l. 257.

l. 658. **ut,** ' how '. **faciem mutatus et ora,** ' changed in appearance and face '. **faciem, ora,** accusatives of respect

l. 659. **furentem,** lit., ' raging ', i.e. ' to madness '. See the note on l. 70 for the proleptic use of the adjective.

l. 660. **ossibus,** ' in her bones ', i.e. ' in her very marrow '. The bones were regarded by the ancients as the seat of feeling and thus the passions were said to feed on them.

ignem. ' The flame ' is the passion of love.

l. 661. **quippe,** ' for, in truth '. For **quippe,** see the note on l. 39.

ambiguam . . bilingues. As a result of the Punic wars during the 3rd century B.C., the Romans came to regard the Carthaginians as treacherous, although there was no basis in actual fact for such a belief. Vergil writing of the foundation of Carthage in about 800 B.C., assigns to Dido and her people the reputation which the Romans attributed to the historic Carthaginians of five centuries later.

l. 662. **urit atrox Iuno**, ' angry Juno chafes (her) ', i.e. ' the anger of Juno . . .' In the *Aeneid*, Juno, queen of heaven, is the sworn enemy of Aeneas and his followers.

l. 664. **meae vires . . . solus.** Take **solus** both with **meae vires** and **potentia**, ' (who art) alone my strength . . .'

l. 665. **patris summi**, i.e. Jupiter, who slew Typhoeus, a monster with a hundred heads, son of Earth, and destined by her to destroy Jupiter for slaying the Titans, also sons of Earth.

tela Typhoëa, ' the bolts such as slew Typhoeus ', lit., ' Typhoean bolts '.

l. 667. **ut**, ' how '. **iactetur**, subjunctive in indirect question, dependent on **nota tibi** with **est** supplied, ' how . . . , is known to thee '. **nota**, nom. pl. neut.

iactetur. The final syllable is lengthened by **ictus**. See the note on l. 651.

l. 669. **dolore nostro**, abl. of cause, ' at my grief '. **nostro** is put for **meo**, as often in poetry.

ll. 671-672. **vereor . . . rerum**, ' I fear whither may end Juno's welcome ; she will not be idle at such a turning-point of fortune '.

Note : (i) the use of **se vertere**, ' to turn (out) ', i.e. ' end '. (ii) ' Juno's welcome '. Juno was the bitter foe of Aeneas and the friend of Carthage. In referring to this welcome as Juno's rather than Dido's, Venus is emphasising the treacherous dangers that exist in his accepting hospitality at Carthage. (iii) **cardo**, lit., ' hinge ', is used metaphorically for ' turning-point '.

l. 673. **cingere flamma**, ' to encircle with (love's) flame '.

l. 674. **ne quo . . . mutet**, ' that she may not change by any (**quo**) power ' = ' that no power may change her '. Venus is again thinking of Juno, who may try to change Dido's love for Aeneas into hatred.

l. 675. **sed . . . amore**, ' but (that) she may be held fast with me in firm love for Aeneas '. Note **Aeneae**, an excellent example of the objective genitive.

l. 676. **qua**, ' how '. **mentem** is ' mind ' in the sense of ' purpose ', ' plan ' ; for **nostram** see l. 669 (note).

l. 677. **accitu** . . . , ' at the summons of his dear father '.

l. 678. **mea maxima cura,** nominative ; therefore in apposition with the subject **regius puer,** and to be translated immediately after those two words.

l. 679. **pelago et flammis** are dependent on **restantia** (in agreement with **dona),** ' surviving (i.e. that survive) the sea and the flames of Troy '.

l. 680. **sopitum somno,** ' lulled in slumber ', in agreement with **hunc. Cytherea.** See the note on l. 257.

l. 681. **sacrata sede,** ablative of place where without a preposition, ' in . . .' Venus means her own temple upon one or other of these mountains.

l. 682. **ne qua,** ' lest in any way ' = ' that in no way '.

mediusve occurrere, ' or come in the middle ' = ' or come between (us) '. The **ob** prefix in **occurrere** expresses the result of such unwanted intervention, ' to my discomfiture '.

l. 683. **noctem** . . . **unam,** ' for not more than one night '.

amplius is often used without **quam** and then has no grammatical influence on the case of the following noun.

l. 684. **falle**, ' imitate'. **puer,** ' boy (as thou art) '. **notos** . . . **vultus,** plural for singular.

l. 686. **regales inter mensas,** ' among the royal tables ', i.e. ' during the royal banquet '. **laticemque Lyaeum,** ' and (amid) the Lyaean liquid '. As Lyaeus (lit., the deliverer from care) was a surname of Bacchus, the phrase means ' flowing wine '.

l. 687. **amplexus,** accusative plural. **figet.** Bring out the full meaning by adding **in ore tuo.**

l. 688. Cupid is to inspire Dido with a deep passion for Aeneas, described by Vergil as ' hidden fire ' and ' poison '.

l. 690. **gressu** goes with **incedit,** ' moves '. **gaudens** suggests Cupid's glee at the trick.

l. 691. **Ascanio.** Translate as the genitive, depending on **per membra.** Such datives, where we expect a possessive, are common.

l. 692. **inrigat,** ' lets . . . flow '.

fotum gremio, ' fondling him in her bosom ' ; lit., ' (him) fondled in her bosom ', object of **tollit.**

dea, ' by her divine power '; lit., ' a goddess ', in apposition with **Venus,** the subject.

l. 694. **aspirans,** lit., ' breathing on (him) ', nominative present participle. Translate as an adjective ' fragrant ' in agreement with **dulci umbra.**

l. 695. **parens,** nominative present participle of **pareo,** ' obedient ', governing the dative **dicto,** here a noun, ' to her command '.

l. 696. **duce laetus Achate,** ' joyful in Achates (as) guide '. **duce Achate,** ablative absolute.

l. 697. **cum,** ' as '. **aulaeis . . . superbis,** ' amid stately curtains ', ' local ' ablative.

l. 698. **sponda=in sponda,** ' local ' abl. again. **mediam** agrees with **se,** (repeated from previous line), object of **locavit,** ' herself middle ', i.e. ' in the midst '. **aurea,** two syllables only, **ea** =one syllable by synaeresis.

l. 700. **discumbitur,** ' (they) recline '. Intransitive verbs are often used impersonally in the passive. Cf. **ventum est,** ' they came '.

strato super ostro, lit., ' on purple laid over ', i.e. ' on purple coverlets '. **Strato** from **sterno.**

l. 701. **manibus,** ' upon their hands '. **dant,** ' pour '.

l. 702. **tonsis mantelia villis,** ' napkins with shorn nap ', i.e. ' smooth-shorn napkins '. They are smooth, not rough and coarse.

ll. 703-704. **famulae,** supply **sunt,** ' there are '. **quibus . . . penates,** lit., ' to whom (is) the task to arrange in order the

long feast and to increase the gods of the store with flames '.
For **quibus cura** say, ' whose task it is '.

This is an obscure passage unless we take **adolere** in its
literal meaning of ' increase ', and the **penates** as ' the gods of
the store ' = ' the hearth-fire ', and the whole of the sentence to
refer to the work of the maids in the kitchen.

l. 705. Supply **sunt** again.   **aetate** is abl. of respect with
pares : ' in age '.

l. 706. **qui . . . onerent . . . ponant.**   Note the subjunctive
mood in the relative clause, expressing purpose.   Render by
English infinitive.

l. 707. **nec non,** ' neither not ' = ' moreover '.   **et,** ' also '.

l. 708. **iussi,** nominative plural perfect participle passive.

toris pictis.   Embroidered couches must mean couches with
embroidered coverlets.

l. 710. **flagrantes . . . vultus,** plural for singular.   **-que . . .
que,** ' both . . . and ', can be ignored in translation.   **flagrantes,**
' glowing '.   The divinity within the pretended Iulus shines
through the human features.

l. 712. **infelix,** ' the unhappy ', is to be taken with **Phoenissa**
(l. 714).   Dido committed suicide after she had failed to
persuade Aeneas to stay with her as her husband and king of
Carthage.

l. 713. **expleri mentem,** ' satisfy her soul '.   **mentem,**
accusative after the passive **expleri,** used in a middle sense.
See the note on l. 228.   **tuendo,** ' with gazing ' = ' as she
gazes '.

l. 715. **ille . . . pependit,** ' when he has hung in the embrace
and on the neck of Aeneas '.   Perhaps we might say, ' hung
in embrace on Aeneas' neck '.   Note the mixture of abstract
and concrete in the words ' embrace ' and ' neck '.

l. 718-719. **haeret,** ' clings (to him) '.   **inscia Dido . . . deus,**
' not knowing, (poor) Dido, how great (is) the god (that)
settles in (her) wretched '.   **miserae,** dative after **insidat,**

(subjunctive in indirect question) may be rendered 'in her, to her misery'.

l. 720. Sychaeus was the uncle and husband of Dido. His murder by Dido's brother, Pygmalion, was the cause of her emigration from her native city Tyre to a new city in N. Africa. **abolere Sychaeum** therefore means 'to efface (the memory of) Sychaeus'.

l. 722. **iam pridem**, = 'now for a long time', which, with **resides** = 'long-dormant'. **desueta corda**, 'heart unused (to love)'.

l. 723. Supply **vēnit** as the verb of **prima quies**, and **sunt** with **remotae** to complete the perfect passive.

l. 724. **vina coronant**. This means what it says, viz., 'surround the bowls with garlands of flowers'. No doubt also, Vergil had in mind a Homeric phrase, 'they wreathed the bowls with wine', i.e. 'they filled them to overflowing'.

l. 725. **vocem volutant**, 'they roll their voices', i.e. 'their voices roll'.

l. 726. For **aureis**, a disyllable by synaeresis, see the note on l. 698.

l. 728. **hic**, adverb, 'hereupon', or better in English, 'then'.

ll. 729-730. **quam . . . soliti**, 'which Belus and all his line (lit., all from Belus) were wont (to fill)'.
Belus, a Phoenician word, meaning 'Lord' and the same word as the Baal and Beelzebub of the Old Testament, is here used to denote the founder of the Tyrian race.

soliti, supply **sunt**, to make the perfect of **soleo, -ere, solitus sum**, semi-deponent.

l. 730. **facta**. Supply **sunt**, and regard this as the perfect of **fio**, 'I happen', 'become'. Here we might say, 'silence fell'.

l. 731. **nam**. The clause beginning with **hospitibus** modifies a missing thought: 'Jupiter (on thee I call), for they say that thou . . .'

ll. 732-733. **velis**, 'mayst thou wish' = 'grant', with

hunc . . . **esse,** as acc. and infin., dependent upon it. **Troiaque profectis,** ' and for-those-who-set-out-from-Troy '. **huius,** supply **diei. minores,** ' descendants '.

l. 734. **adsit,** ' optative ' subjunctive, expressing a wish : ' may . . .' **bona,** ' kindly ', or ' bounteous '.

l. 735. **celebrate faventes,** ' attend favouring ' = ' honour with your friendly presence '.

l. 736. **laticum libavit honorem,** lit., ' she poured out an offering of liquids (=of wine) '. Translate, ' she offered libation of wine '.

l. 737. **libato,** ablative absolute in one word, lit., ' the libation having been offered ' = ' after the libation '.

summo tenus attigit ore, ' she touched (the goblet) as far as the lips (lit., the edge of her mouth) '. **Tenus** is a preposition governing the ablative case. The expression seems awkward but the sense is clear, if we render, ' merely with her lips '.

prima is emphatic : ' she was the first to touch '.

l. 738. **impiger,** adj. for adv.

l. 739. **pleno . . . auro,** lit., ' steeped himself in the brimming gold ', a vigorous expression to mark a contrast between the manly drinking of Bitias and the dainty sip of Dido.

l. 740. **post,** adverb.

l. 741. **personat,** ' makes (the halls) resound '. **maximus,** ' mighty '.

The story is well known how Atlas rebelled with the other Titans against Zeus, was defeated, and condemned to bear heaven and earth on his head and shoulders. A later tradition, which Vergil seems to be following here, states that he was a philosopher and astronomer and that the African mountains were named after him.

ll. 742-746. The theme of Iopas' songs is nature and her secrets. Vergil was a keen student of philosophy, and a great admirer of the Roman poet Lucretius, who had expounded the philosophy of Epicurus in his great work ' On the Nature of

Things '. Thus it is natural for him to attribute to Iopas his own love for the study of nature.

l. 742. **canit,** 'sings of '. **solisque labores,** 'the sufferings of the sun ', are best explained as eclipses.

l. 743. **unde** ... Supply the verb 'spring' or 'arise'. **ignes,** i.e. lightning.

l. 744. **Arcturum ... Triones,** accusatives after **canit,** l. 742, which should be repeated here in translation. Arcturus is the brightest star in the constellation Boötes. Its rising and setting were considered by the ancients to bring in bad weather.

The **Hyades** (lit., 'rainy stars ') are another constellation whose morning rising in May ushered in the rains of spring.

Triones is the constellation of the Great Bear. **Gemini Triones** include both the Great and the Little Bear.

l. 745. **quid,** 'why '. **tantum,** adverbial accusative, 'so much '.

l. 746. **vel quae,** etc., i.e. why the nights of winter are so long. **obstet,** like **properent,** l. 745, is subjunctive in an indirect question.

l. 747. **ingeminant plausu,** 'redouble with their applause ' = 'applaud again and again '.

l. 748. **nec non et.** See note on l. 707.

l. 749. **longum bibebat amorem,** 'drank long love ' or as we say, 'drank deeply of love '.

l. 751. **Aurorae filius** is Memnon, for whom see the note on l. 489. **venisset** is subjunctive in indirect question, dependent on 'she asked '. easily supplied from **rogitans,** l. 751.

l. 752. **nunc quales ... Achilles,** lit., 'now (she asked) what kind of horses (were) Diomede's, now, how great (was) Achilles ' ; i.e. 'she asked now of the nature of Diomede's horses, now of the greatness of Achilles '.

Diomedes is one of the great heroes on the Greek side in the Trojan war. The fifth book of the *Iliad* is devoted almost exclusively to his exploits, which include severely wounding

Aeneas and stealing his ' sleek-coated ' horses. Again in the twenty-third book, he is the victor in an exciting chariot-race.

In view of these facts, commentators seem to think that it is rather tactless of Dido to ask questions of Aeneas concerning Diomede and his horses, and Page in his edition writes quite seriously of ladies who when indulging in indiscriminate enquiries often make slips. Surely, however, there is no difficulty : there is no reason to suppose that Dido would have been familiar with all the details of the Trojan war ; hence she quite naturally asks about the first persons that occur to her, and they will be the two most famous warriors on the Greek side, Diomede and Achilles.

l. 753. **age.** See note on **agite,** l. 627.

l. 754. **insidias Danaum,** ' the wiles of the Greeks ' is a reference to the trick of the wooden horse by which the Greeks captured Troy.

tuorum, ' of thy comrades '.

l. 756. **septima aestas,** ' the seventh summer '. During his seven years' wandering over the Mediterranean after his flight from Troy in search of the promised land, Aeneas had visited Thrace, Crete, Epirus (modern Albania), Sicily, and finally Carthage. He tells Dido the story of his wanderings (**errores**) in Book III after he has described Troy's last days in Book II. **omnibus terris et fluctibus,** ' local ' abl. with **errantem,** ' over every land and sea '.

VOCABULARY

(N.B.—In the following vocabulary the figures (1), (2), (3), (4), *after the verbs, denote the conjugation. No conjugation number is given in the case of* -io *verbs like* capio. *Verbs followed only by a conjugation number, no principal parts being given, are regular.*

ā, ab, *prep. with abl.*, from, by.

Abas, -antis, *m.*, Abas (*companion of Aeneas*).

abdō, -ere, -didī, -ditum (3), hide.

abeō, -īre, -iī, -itum, go away, depart.

aboleō, -ēre, -ēvī, -itum (2), blot out, efface.

abripiō, -ere, -ripuī, -reptum, snatch away, tear, carry off.

absistō, -ere, -stitī (3), stay, stop ; desist.

absum, -esse, āfuī, am away *or* absent ; am distant.

absūmō, -ere, -sūmpsī, -sūmptum (3), take away, destroy.

ac, and.

acanthus, -ī, *m.*, acanthus.

accēdō, -ere, -cessī, -cessum (3), approach, come to.

accendō, -ere, -ndī, -nsum (3), inflame, kindle.

accingō, -ere, -nxī, -nctum (3), gird.

accipiō, -ere, -cēpī, -ceptum, receive, take ; let in (123) ; welcome (290), hear (676).

accītus, -ūs, *m.*, summons.

accumbō, -ere, -cubuī, -cubitum (3), recline at.

ācer, ācris, ācre, sharp, fierce, bold.

acerbus, -a, -um, bitter, harsh.

Acestēs, -ae, *m.*, Acestes (*mythical king of Sicily*).

Achātēs, -ae, *m.*, Achates (*companion of Aeneas*).

Achillēs, -ī, *m.*, Achilles.

Achīvī, -ōrum, *m. pl.*, Greeks.

Acīdalius, -a, -um, Acidalian (*epithet of Venus*).

aciēs, -ēī, *f.*, line ; troop.

āctus, *see* ago.

acūtus, -a, -um, sharp.

ad, *prep. with acc.*, to, towards.

addō, -ere, -didī, -ditum (3), add, give.

adeō, -īre, -iī, -itum, go to, approach.

adeō, *adverb*, to such an extent.

adflīgō, -ere, -flīxī, -flīctum (3), afflict, trouble, vex.

adflō (1), breathe upon, shed.

adfor (1 *dep.*), speak to, address.

adhūc, *adv.*, yet, hitherto.

adloquor, -ī, -locūtus sum (3 *dep.*), speak to, address.

adnītor, -nītī, -nīxus sum (3 *dep.*), toil, heave.

adnō (1), swim to.

adnuō, -ere, -uī (3), allow, grant.

adoleō, -ēre, -uī, (2), honour ; increase (704).

adōrō (1), worship, revere.

129

adsum, -esse, -fuī, am present, am near.

adsurgō, -ere, -surrēxī, -surrectum (3), rise up.

adultus, -a, -um, full grown.

advehō, -ere, -xī, -ctum (3), bring to, carry to ; *in pass.*, sail to (558).

adveniō, -īre, -vēnī, -ventum (4), come to, arrive at, reach, visit.

adversus, -a, -um, facing, opposite, in front of.

Aeacidēs, -ae, *m.*, son *or* descendant of Aeacus = Achilles.

aeger, -gra, -grum, sick.

Aenĕadae, -um, *m. pl.*, followers of Aeneas.

Aenēās, -ae, *m.*, Aeneas.

aēnum, -ī, *n.*, bronze vessel.

aēnus, -a, -um, of bronze.

Aeolia, -ae, *f.*, Aeolia (*an island*).

Aeolus, -ī, *m.*, Aeolus (*god of the winds*).

aequō, (1), make equal, match.

aequor, -is, *n.*, sea.

aequus, -a, -um, equal, fair ; favourable.

āēr, -is, *m.*, air ; mist.

aereus, -a, -um, of bronze.

aes, aeris, *n.*, bronze.

aestās, -ātis, *f.*, summer.

aestus, -ūs, *m.*, tide, surge.

aetās, -ātis, *f.*, age.

aeternus, -a, -um, eternal, everlasting.

aethēr, -is, *m.* (*acc. sg.* aethera), (*upper*) air ; sky, heaven.

aetherius, -a, -um, heavenly, ethereal.

Āfricus, -ī, *m.*, South Wind.

age, *imperative* of ago, come!

Agēnor, -oris, *m.*, Agenor (*ancestor of Dido.*)

ager, agrī, *m.*, land, field.

agger, -is, *m.*, pile, heap, mound.

āgmen, -inis, *n.*, line ; band, troop.

āgnōscō, -ere, -nōvī, -nitum (3), recognize, know.

āgnus, -ī, *m.*, lamb.

agō, -ere, ēgī, āctum (3), drive ; harass (240) ; do, perform ; treat (574) ; age, *imperative,* come!

Āiax, -ācis, *m.*, Ajax.

aiō, say, speak.

āla, -ae, *f.*, wing.

Alba, -ae, *f.*, Alba.

Albānus, -a, -um, of Alba, Alban.

āles, -itis, *c.*, bird.

Alētēs, -ī, *m.*, Aletes (*a Trojan*).

āliger, -era, -erum, winged.

aliquī, -qua, -quod, *adj.*, some, any.

aliquis, -quid, *pron.*, some one, anyone.

aliter, *adv.*, otherwise.

alius, -a, -ud, other, another ; aliī . . . aliī, some . . . others.

alligō (1), bind, hold fast.

almus, -a, -um, gentle, kind, kindly ; gracious (618).

altē, *adv.*, high, on high.

alter, -era, -erum, one *or* the other (*of two*) ; another.

altum, -ī, *n.*, the deep, the sea.

altus, -a, -um, high, deep.

amāns, -antis, *c.*, lover.

amāracus, -ī, *m.*, marjoram.

Amāzonides, -um, *f. pl.*, Amazons.

ambāgēs, -is, *f.*, a going about.

ambiguus, -a, -um, doubtful, treacherous.

ambo, -ae, -o, both.

ambrosius, -a, -um, ambrosial.

amictus, -ūs, *m.*, cloak, mantle.

amictus, -a, -um, clad, shrouded.

amīcus, -ī, *m.*, friend.

āmittō, -ere, -mīsī, -missum (3), lose.

amor, -ōris, *m.*, love, longing, passion.

amplexus, -ūs, *m.*, embrace.

amplius, *adv.*, more, further.

amplus, -a, -um, large, wide; spacious (725).

Amycus, -ī, *m.*, Amycus (*a Trojan*).

Anchīsēs, -ae, *m.*, Anchises (*father of Aeneas*).

ancora, -ae, f., anchor.

anima, -ae, *f.*, spirit, life.

animus, -ī, *m.*, mind, soul, spirit, feeling; disposition (304); *pl.*, rage.

annālēs, -ium, *m. pl.*, record, story.

annus, -ī, *m.*, year.

ante, *prep. with acc.*, before; *adv.*, before, earlier, sooner.

Antēnor, -oris, *m.*, Antenor (*a Trojan*).

Antheus (*acc.* Anthea), *m.*, Antheus (*a Trojan*).

antīquus, -a, -um, ancient, old.

antrum, -ī, *n.*, cavern.

aper, aprī, *m.*, wild boar.

aperiō, -īre, -uī, apertum (4), open, reveal.

apertus, -a, -um, open; cloudless (155).

apis, -is, *f.*, bee.

appāreō (2), appear, am seen.

appellō, -ere, -pulī, appulsum (3), bring.

applicō, -āre, āvī *or* uī, -ātum *or* -itum (1), bring.

aptō (1), fit, fashion; shape (552).

aqua, -ae, *f.*, water; spring (167).

Aquilō, -ōnis, *m.*, North Wind.

āra, -ae, *f.*, altar.

arbor, -is, *f.*, tree.

arboreus, -a, -um, of a tree; branching (190).

arcānum, -ī, *n.*, secret.

arceō, -ēre, -uī, arctum (2), keep off, bar, keep away.

Arctūrus, -ī, *m.*, Arcturus (*brightest star in Bootes*).

arcus, -ūs, *m.*, bow.

ārdeō, -ēre, ārsī (2), burn (*intrans.*), am hot; am eager (515), am busy.

ārdescō, -ere (3), am inflamed (*with love*).

argentum, -ī, *n.*, silver.

Argī, -ōrum, *m. pl.*, Argos (*a Greek city in Peloponnese*).

Argīvī, -ōrum, *m. pl.*, Greeks.

Argīvus, -a, -um, Argive *or* Greek.

Argos (*only in nom. and acc.*), *n.*, Argos.

āridus, -a, -um, dry.

arma, -ōrum, *n. pl.*, arms, implements.

armentum, -ī, *n.*, herd.

arrēctus, -a, -um, alert, attentive; cheered, encouraged (579).

ars, artis, *f.*, skill.

artifex, -icis, *m.*, artist, workman.

artus, -a, -um, close, tight (293).

artus, -ūs, *m.*, limb.

arvum, -ī, *n.*, field, land.

arx, arcis, *f.*, fortress, citadel, tower.

Ascanius, -ī, *m.*, Ascanius (*son of Aeneas*).

ascendō, -ere, -dī, -sum, (3), climb, mount.

Asia, -ae, *f.*, Asia.

aspectō (1), look on, gaze at.

aspectus, -ūs, *m.*, look, glance; countenance; sight (613).

asper, -era, -erum, rough, fierce, wild, savage; formidable; resentful (279).

aspiciō, -ere, -ēxī, -ectum, look, see; regard (526).

aspīrō, (1), breathe on.

Assaracus, -ī, *m.*, Assaracus (*a Trojan king*).

ast, but.

astō, -āre, astitī (1), stand near; alight (301).

astrum, -ī, *n.*, star.

at, but.

āter, ātra, ātrum, black.

Atlās, -antis, *m.*, Atlas (*philosopher and hero*).

atque, and.

Atrīdae, -ārum, *m. pl.*, sons of Atreus (*Agamemnon and Menelaus*).

ātrium, -ī, *n.*, hall.

ātrōx, -ōcis, fierce, dread.

attingō, -ere, -tigī, -tāctum, (3), touch.

attollō, -ere (3), lift up, raise.

audeō, -ēre, ausus sum (2 *semidep.*), dare, venture.

audiō, (4), hear.

augurium, -ī, *n.*, augury, prophecy.

aula, -ae, *f.*, court.

aulaea, -ōrum, *n. pl.*, curtains.

aura, -ae, *f.*, breeze, air.

aurātus, -a, -um, gilt, gilded.

aureus, -a, -um, golden.

auris, -is, *f.*, ear.

Aurōra, -ae, *f.*, Aurora (*goddess of the dawn*); dawn.

aurum, -ī, *n.*, gold.

Auster, -trī, *m.*, South Wind.

ausus, *see* audeō.

aut, or; aut . . . aut, either . . . or

auxilium, -ī, *n.*, help, aid.

avārus, -a, -um, greedy, niggardly, grasping.

āvehō, -ere, -ēxī, -ectum (3), carry away.

āversus, -a, -um, distant.

āvertō, -ere, -rtī, -rsum (3), turn aside *or* away (472, 482), turn round.

avidus, -a, -um, eager.

bācātus, -a, -um, of pearls.

Bacchus, -ī, *m.*, Bacchus (734); wine.

barbarus, -a, -um, savage.

beātus, -a, -um, happy, blest.

bellātrīx, -īcis, *f.*, woman warrior.

bellō, (1), fight, wage war, war.

bellum, -ī, *n.*, war.

Bēlus, -ī, *m.*, Belus (*king of Sidon*).

benīgnus, -a, -um, kind, kindly.

bibō, -ere, bibī (3), drink.

bilinguis, -e, double-tongued, deceitful.

bīnī, -ae, -a, two each, two.

birēmis, -is, *f.*, bireme, galley (*properly, ship with two banks of oars*).

bis, *adv.*, twice.

Bitias, -ae, *m.*, Bitias (*courtier of Dido*).

blandus, -a, -um, soft, soothing; flattering.

bonus, -a, -um, good, kind; bounteous (734).

brevia, -ium, *n. pl.*, shallows, shoals.

breviter, *adv.*, shortly, briefly.

Byrsa, -ae, *f.*, Byrsa (*citadel of Carthage*).

cadō, -ere, cecidī, cāsum (3), fall, sink.

cadus, -ī, *m.*, jar.

caecus, -a, -um, blind ; unseen ; hidden (536).

caedēs, -is, *f.*, slaughter, carnage.

caelestis, -e, heavenly, divine ; *as noun*, heavenly ones, the gods.

caelō (1), carve.

caelum, -ī, *n.*, heaven, sky.

Caesar, -is, *m.*, Caesar.

caesariēs, -ēī, *f.*, flowing locks.

Caīcus, -ī, *m.*, Caicus (*companion of Aeneas*).

caleō (2), am hot, glow.

campus, -ī, *m.*, plain, field.

canistrum, -ī, *n.*, basket.

canō, -ere, cecinī, cantum (3), sing.

cantus, -ūs, *m.*, song.

cānus, -a, -um, white-haired, hoary.

capessō, -ere, -īvī, -ītum (3), take in hand, perform.

capiō, -ere, cēpī, captum, take, catch, choose.

caput, -itis, *n.*, head.

Capys, *acc.*, Capyn, *m.*, Capys (*a Trojan*).

carcer, -is, *m.*, prison.

cardō, -inis, *m.*, hinge ; turning point (672).

carpō, -ere, -psī, -ptum (3), pluck, take ; enjoy, breathe (388).

cārus, -a, -um, dear.

castra, -ōrum, *n. pl.*, camp.

cāsus, -ūs, *m.*, chance ; hazard (9, 204) ; fate (221) ; mischance, misfortune (599, 614).

caterva, -ae, *f.*, troop, band, crowd.

causa, -ae, *f.*, cause.

cavātus, -a, -um, hollow.

cavō, (1), hollow out.

cavus, -a, -um, hollow ; enfolding (516).

cecidī, *see* cadō.

celebrō (1), attend, celebrate.

celer, -is, -e, quick, swift.

celerō (1), hasten, speed.

cella, -ae, *f.*, cell.

cēlō, (1), hide.

celsus, -a, -um, high, lofty.

centum, a hundred.

Cereālis, -e, of Ceres.

Cerēs, -eris, *f.*, Ceres ; corn, bread.

cernō, -ere, crēvī, crētum (3), see, discern.

certē, *adv.*, surely, certainly ; at least.

certō, (1), strive, contend, vie.

certus, -a, -um, fixed, sure : trusty (576).

cervīx, -īcis, *f.*, neck.

cervus, -ī, *m.*, stag.

cessō, (1), linger ; am idle (672).

cēterī, -ae, -a, the other, the rest (of).

chorus, -ī, *m.*, dance.

cieō, -ēre, cīvī, citum (2), rouse.

cingō, -ere, -nxī, -nctum (3), gird, surround ; circle (*the sky*).

cingulum, -ī, *n.*, belt.

circum, *adv.*, around ; *prep. with acc.*, round, about.

circumdō, -are, -dedī, -datum (1), surround, enclose.

circumfundō, -ere, -fūdī, -fūsum (3), shed round, enfold.

circumfūsus, -a, -um, surrounding, encircling.

circumtextus, -a, -um, broidered.

cithara, -ae, *f.*, harp, lyre.

citius, *adv.*, more swiftly.

citus, -a, -um, quick, swift.

clam, *adv.*, secretly, by stealth.

clāmor, -ōris, *m.*, shout, shouting, clamour.

clārus, -a, -um, clear, bright; great, famous.

classis, -is, *f.*, fleet.

claudō, -ere, -sī, -sum (3), shut, close.

claustrum, -ī, barrier, bar, bolt.

Cloanthus, -ī, *m.*, Cloanthus (*a Trojan*).

coepī, -isse, *defective vb.*, began.

coetus, -ūs, *m.*, crowd, gathering (735), flock.

cōgnōmen, -inis, *n.*, name, surname.

cōgnōscō, -ere, -nōvī, -nitum (3), learn, know.

cōgō, -ere, coēgī, coāctum (3), compel, constrain.

colligō, -ere, -lēgī, -lectum (3), gather, collect.

collis, -is, *m.*, hill.

collum, -ī, *n.*, neck.

colō, -ere, coluī, cultum (3), till (532); frequent, visit; love (16).

colōnus, -ī, *m.*, settler.

columna, -ae, *f.*, pillar.

coma, -ae, *f.*, hair.

comitātus, -a, -um, accompanied.

commissum, -ī, *n.*, deed, fault.

committō, -ere, -mīsī, -missum (3), commit.

commoveō, -ēre, -mōvī, -mōtum (2), move, disturb, excite.

compāgēs, -is, *f.*, joint; fastening, bolt.

compāgō, -inis, *f.*, joint.

compellō, (1), accost, address.

compellō, -ere, -pulī, -pulsum (3), drive, force.

complector, -tī, -xus sum (3 *dep.*), embrace, clasp.

complexus, -ūs, *m.*, embrace, clasp.

compōnō, -ere, -posuī, -positum (3), settle, order; abate, quiet, lay to rest; lay (698).

compostus, -a, -um (=compositus), settled.

conciliō, (1), win over, make favourable; win, gain (79).

conclūdō, -ere, -sī, -sum (3), enclose.

concurrō, -ere, -currī, -cursum (3), charge; meet in battle.

concursus, -ūs, *m.*, gathering, crowd.

condō, -ere, -didī, -ditum (3), build, found.

cōnfīdō, -ere, -fīsus sum (3 *semidep. with dative*), trust.

cōnfugiō, -ere, -fūgī, fly for refuge.

congredior, -ī, -gressus sum (*dep.*), meet, am matched with.

coniungō, -ere, -nxī, -nctum (3), join, unite.

coniunx, -iugis, *c.*, wife, husband, spouse.

cōnscendō, -ere, -ndī, -nsum (3), mount, climb.

cōnscius, -a, -um, conscious.

cōnsīdō, -ere, -sēdī, -sessum (3), settle.

cōnsilium, -ī, *n.*, plan, counsel, resolve.

cōnsistō, -ere, -stitī (3), stand ; rest (643), find rest (629), am still ; halt (187).

cōnspectus, -ūs, *m.*, sight.

cōnspiciō, -ere, -spexī, -spectum, see, catch sight of.

cōnstituō, -ere, -uī, -ūtum (3), arrange, determine.

contendō, -ere, -ndī, -ntum (3), strive ; press on, hasten (158).

contingō, -ere, -tigī, -tāctum (3), touch ; fall to one's lot, befall.

contrā, *adv.*, opposite ; on the other hand ; in answer (76) ; *prep. with acc.*, against, opposite to.

contrārius, -a, -um, contrary, opposed.

contundō, -ere, -tudī, -tūsum *or* tūnsum (3), crush.

cōnūbium, -ī, *n.*, marriage.

convellō, -ere, -vellī, vulsum (3), tear, wrench ; shatter.

conveniō, -īre, -vēnī, -ventum (4), come together, assemble.

convertō, -ere, -rtī, -rsum (3), turn round, turn, reverse.

convexum, -ī, *n.*, vault, arch ; slope (608).

convīvium, -ī, *n.*, feast, banquet.

coorior, -īrī, -ortus sum (4 *dep.*), arise.

cōpia, -ae, *f.*, leave, licence, chance.

cor, cordis, *n.*, heart.

cōram, *adv.*, face to face.

cornū, -ūs, *n.*, horn.

corōna, -ae, *f.*, crown.

corōnō, (1), crown.

corpus, -oris, *n.*, body, carcase.

corripiō, -ere, -ripuī, -reptum, seize, snatch, catch up.

corrumpō, -ere, -rūpī, -ruptum (3), spoil.

coruscus, -a, -um, waving.

costa, -ae, *f.*, rib.

coturnus, -ī, *m.*, buskin, hunting-boot.

crātēr, -ēris, *m.*, bowl (*for mixing wine*).

crēber, -bra, -brum, frequent.

crēdō, -ere, -didī, -ditum (3), believe.

crīnēs, -ium, *m. pl.*, hair.

crīnītus, -a, -um, long-haired.

crispō, (1), shake, wave ; grasp (313).

cristātus, -a, -um, crested.

croceus, -a, -um, yellow.

crūdēlis, -e, cruel, pitiless ; bitter (361).

cruentus, -a, -um, bloody, blood-stained.

cum, *prep. with abl.*, with.

cum, *conj.*, when ; since, as.

cumulus, -ī, *m.*, heap, pile.

cunctus, -a, -um, all.

Cupīdō, -inis, *m.*, Cupid.

cūr, why.

cūra, -ae, *f.*, care, anxiety, trouble.

currō, -ere, cucurrī, cursum (3), run.

currus, -ūs, *m.*, car, chariot.

cursus, -ūs, *m.*, course, flight.

cuspis, -idis, *f.*, spear, lance.

custōs, -ōdis, *m.*, guard.

Cyclōpius, -a, -um, of the Cyclops.

cycnus, -ī, *m.*, swan.

Cȳmothoē, *f.*, Cymothoë

Cynthus, -ī, *m.*, (Mt.) Cynthus.

Cyprus, -i, *f.*, Cyprus.

Cythēra, -ōrum, *n. pl.*, Cythera.

Cytherēa, -ae, *f.*, she of Cythera, i.e. Venus.

Danaī, -um, *m. pl.*, Greeks.

dapēs, -um, *f. pl.*, feast.

Dardanidae, -um, *m. pl.*, Trojans.

Dardanius, -a, -um, Trojan.

dator, -ōris, *m.*, giver.

dē, *prep. with abl.*, from; concerning; after (277); according to (318).

dea, -ae, *f.*, goddess.

decōrus, -a, -um, beautiful.

decus, -oris, *n.*, beauty, adornment.

dēfessus, -a, -um, weary, worn out.

dēfīgō, -ere, -fīxī, -fixum (3), cast down, fix.

dēfīxus, -a, -um, downcast, fixed.

dēfluō, -ere, -xī (3), flow down.

dehinc, *adv.*, then.

dehīscō, -ere (3), gape.

deīnde, *adv.*, then, after that.

Dēiopēa, -ae, *f.*, Deiopea.

dēmittō, -ere, -mīsī, -missum (3), send down; hand down (288); cast down (561).

dēmum, *adv.*, at length.

dēnī, -ae, -a, ten each, ten.

dēpendeō, -ēre, (2) hang down.

dērigō, -ere, rēxī, -rēctum, (3), direct.

dēsertum, -ī, *n.*, desert.

dēsistō, -ere, -stitī, -stitum (3), cease, forbear.

dēspectō, (1), look down on.

dēspiciō, -ere, -spēxī, -spectum, look down on.

dēsuētus, -a, -um, unused.

dēsuper, *adv.*, from above; above.

dētrūdō, -ere, -ūsī, -ūsum (3), thrust off.

deus, -ī, *m.*, god.

dēveniō, -īre, -vēnī, -ventum (4), come down to, reach.

dēvoveō, -ēre, -vōvī, -vōtum (2), devote, doom.

dextera *or* dextra, -ae, *f.*, right hand.

dī, *nom. pl.* of deus.

Diāna, -ae, *f.*, Diana.

diciō, -ōnis, *f.*, sovereignty.

dicō, (1), dedicate, proclaim; make (73).

dīcō, -ere, -xī, -ctum (3), say, tell; name, call (530).

dictum, -ī, *n.*, word, utterance, speech.

Dīdō, -ōnis, *f.*, Dido.

diēs, -ēī, *m., rarely f.*, day; (*gen. sg.* diī, 636).

diffundō, -ere, -fūdī, -fūsum (3), spread, scatter, shed abroad.

dignor, (1 *dep.*), deem worthy.

dīgnus, -a, -um, worthy.

dīligō, -ere, -lēxī, -lēctum (3), love.

dīmittō, -ere, -mīsī, -missum (3), send away, send off.

Diomēdēs, -is, *m.*, Diomedes.

dīrigō, -ere, -rēxī, -rēctum (3), direct.

dīripiō, -ere, -ripuī, -reptum, strip.

dīrus, -a, -um, dire, dread.

discō, -ere, didicī (3), learn.

discrīmen, -inis, *n.*, danger, crisis; distinction (574).

discumbō, -ere, -cubuī, -cubitum (3), recline.

dīsiciō, -ere, -iēci, -iectum, shatter, scatter.

disiungō, -ere, -iunxī, -iunctum (3), separate, part, keep away.

dispellō, -ere, -pulī, -pulsum (3), scatter.

dissimulō, (1), hide (*feelings*), dissemble.

distendō, -ere, -ndī, -ntum (3), stretch, swell out.

dītissimus, -a, -um, *superl. of* dīves, richest.

diū, *adv.*, for a long time, long.

dīva, -ae, *f.*, goddess.

dīversus, -a, -um, far off, distant ; separate ; this way and that (70).

dīves, -itis, rich.

dīvidō, -ere, -īsī, -īsum (3), divide, cleave ; share out.

dīvīnus -a, -um, divine, godlike.

dīvus, -ī, *gen. pl.* dīvum, *m.*, god.

dō, dare, dedī, datum (1), give ; allow (409) ; put, place, make ; dispense (29) ; dare vēla, set sail.

doceō, -ēre, -cuī, -ctum (2), teach, tell.

doleō, -ēre, -uī, -itum (2), grieve.

dolor, -ōris, *m.*, grief, sorrow, resentment, pain.

dolus, -ī, *m.*, guile, craft, wile.

dominor, (1 *dep.*), rule.

dominus, -ī, *m.*, lord, master.

domus, -ūs, *f.*, house, home ; *locative*, domī.

dōnec, until ; while.

dōnum, -ī, *n.*, gift, offering.

dorsum, -ī, *n.*, back, ridge.

dubitō, (1), doubt, hesitate.

dubius, -a, -um, doubtful, hesitating, wavering.

dūcō, -ere, -xī, -ctum (3), lead, draw, bring ; *with* mūrōs, build (423).

ductor, -ōris, *m.*, leader.

dūdum, *adv.*, long since.

dulcis, -e, sweet, dear ; of fresh water (167).

dum, while, until.

duplex, -icis, double ; both.

dūrō, (1), endure, hold out.

dūrus, -a, -um, hard.

dux, ducis, *m.*, leader, guide, chief, general.

ē *or* ex, *prep. with abl.*, out of, from ; in accordance with.

ebur, eboris, *n.*, ivory.

ēdūcō, -ere, -xī, -ctum (3), lead out.

efferō, -ferre, extulī, ēlātum, carry out ; raise ; bring forth (652).

efficiō, -ere, -fēcī, -fectum, make, form.

effodiō, -ere, -fōdī, -fossum, dig out.

effundō, -ere, -fūdī, -fūsum (3), pour out, shed.

egēnus, -a, -um, destitute.

egeō, -ēre, -uī (2), am in want.

ego, I.

ēgredior, -ī, -gressus sum, go out, step forth, disembark.

ēgregius, -a, -um, noble, famous, great.

ēiciō, -ere, -iēcī, -iectum, cast out, drive out.

ēlābor, -ī, -lapsus sum (3), slip away, escape.

ēmittō, -ere, -mīsī, -missum (3), send out, let go ; let loose (125).

ēn, lo! behold'

enim, for ; **sed enim**, but indeed.
eō, **īre**, **iī**, **itum**, go, pass.
Eōus, **-a**, **-um**, Eastern.
epulae, **-ārum**, *f. pl.*, feast.
equidem, *adv.*, certainly, at least.
equus, **-ī**, *m.*, horse.
ēripiō, **-ere**, **-ripuī**, **-reptum** (3), take away, snatch away ; save, rescue (596).
errō, (1), wander.
error, **-ōris**, *m.*, wandering ; error.
ērumpō, **-ere**, **-rūpī**, **-ruptum** (3), break out, burst forth.
Eryx, **-ycis**, *m.*, Eryx.
et, and, also, even ; **et . . . et**, both . . . and.
etiam, besides, also, even.
Eurōpa, **-ae**, *f.*, Europe.
Eurōtas, **-ae**, *m.*, Eurotas.
Eurus, **-ī**, *m.*, East Wind.
ēvertō, **-ere**, **-rtī**, **-rsum** (3), over-turn ; overthrow, destroy ; stir up (43).
ex, *see* **ē**.
exanimus, **-a**, **-um**, lifeless.
exaudiō, (4), hear.
excēdō, **-ere**, **-cessī**, **-cessum** (3), depart, leave.
excidium, **-ī**, *n.*, ruin, destruc-tion.
excidō, **-ere**, **-cidī** (3), fall from, fall out ; fade (26).
excīdō, **-ere**, **-cīdī**, **-cīsum** (3), cut out, quarry.
excipiō, **-ere**, **-cēpī**, **-ceptum**, take up, succeed to.
excūdō, **-ere**, **-cūdī**, **-cūsum** (3), strike out.
excutiō, **-ere**, **-cussī**, **-cussum**, shake off.
exeō, **-īre**, **-iī**, **-itum**, go out, depart.

exerceō, (2), practise (499) ; set to work, make busy (431).
exhauriō, **-īre**, **-hausī**, **-haustum** (4), draw out, wear out.
exigō, **-ere**, **-ēgī**, **-āctum** (3), complete ; pass, spend (*time*).
eximō, **-ere**, **-ēmī**, **-ēmptum** (3), take away.
expediō, (4), get ready, serve.
expellō, **-ere**, **-pulī**, **-pulsum** (3), drive out.
experior, **-īrī**, **-pertus sum** (4 *dep.*), try ; know.
expleō, **-ēre**, **-ēvī**, **-ētum** (2), fill up, complete ; satisfy (713).
explōrō, (1), search out, explore.
exserō, **-ere**, **-ruī**, **-rtum** (3), put forth, display.
exsilium, **-ī**, *n.*, exile.
exspīrō, (1), breathe out, gasp out.
extemplō, *adv.*, at once, forth-with.
extrēmus, **-a**, **-um**, furthest, last, extreme.
extulī, *see* **effero**.
exuō, **-ere**, **-uī**, **-ūtum** (3), put off ; shed.
exūro, **-ere**, **-ussī**, **-ustum** (3), burn up.

faciēs, **-ēī**, *f.*, face ; appearance.
facilis, **-e**, easy.
faciō, **-ere**, **fēcī**, **factum**, do, make, perform.
factum, **-ī**, *n.*, deed.
fallō, **-ere**, **fefellī**, **falsum** (3), deceive ; feign, imitate (684).
falsus, **-a**, **-um**, false.
fāma, **-ae**, *f.*, fame, glory ; reputation ; rumour, tale.
famēs, **-is**, *f.*, hunger, famine.
famula, **-ae**, *f.*, handmaid.

famulus, -i, *m.*, slave, servant.

fandum, -i, *n.*, right.

fās, *n.* (*indeclinable*), right, lawful.

fastīgium, -i, *n.*, top, summit.

fatīgō, (1), weary, trouble, tire out.

fatīscō, -ere (3), gape.

fātum, -i, *n.*, fate ; doom, destiny.

fātur, *see* for.

faveō, -ēre, fāvī, fautum (2), favour (*often with dative.*)

fax, facis, *f.*, torch.

fēlīx, -icis, happy, fortunate.

fēmina, -ae, *f.*, woman.

fera, -ae, *f.*, wild beast.

ferīna, -ae, *f.*, beast's flesh, venison.

feriō, -ire (4), strike.

ferō, ferre, tulī, lātum, bear, carry, bring ; endure ; give birth to (605) ; receive ; carry off (59) ; say, relate (645), tell of (625) ; mē ferō, move, advance, approach.

ferōx, -ōcis, spirited ; warlike (302) ; proud, stubborn.

ferrum, -i, *n.*, iron ; sword.

ferveō, -ēre, ferbuī (2), am aglow.

fessus, -a, -um, weary.

fētus, -a, -um, full, teeming.

fētus, -ūs, *m.*, offspring.

Fidēs, -eī, *f.*, Faith.

fīdūcia, -ae, *f.*, confidence, pride.

fīdus, -a, -um, faithful, trusty.

fīgō, -ere, -xī, -xum (3), fix ; pierce ; imprint (687).

fīlius, -i, *m.*, son.

fīnis, -is, *m.*, end, bound ; *in pl.*, frontiers, lands.

fīō, fierī, factus sum, arise.

flagrō, (1), glow.

flamma, -ae, *f.*, flame, fire

flammātus, -a, -um, burning.

flāvus, -a, -um, yellow.

flectō, -ere, -xī, -xum (3), turn, wheel (*transitive*).

flōreus, -a, -um, flowery.

flōs, flōris, *m.*, flower.

fluctus, -ūs, *m.*, wave, billow.

flūmen, -inis, *n.*, river, stream.

fluō, -ere, -xī (3), flow.

fluvius, -i, *m.*, river, stream.

foedus, -eris, *n.*, treaty ; covenant (62) ; bond, law.

folium, -i, *n.*, leaf.

fōmes, -itis, *m.*, tinder.

fōns, fontis, *m.*, fount, spring, stream ; source (244).

for, fārī, fātus sum (1 *dep.*), speak, say.

fore, *fut. infin. of* sum.

forēs, -um, *f. pl.*, doors.

forma, -ae, *f.*, form, beauty.

fors, -tis, *f.*, chance.

forsan, *adv.*, perhaps.

forte, *adv.*, by chance ; perhaps.

fortis, -e, strong, brave.

fortūna, -ae, *f.*, fortune, luck.

fortūnātus, -a, -um, happy, lucky, blest.

foveō, -ēre, fōvī, fōtum (2), cherish, foster ; fondle (718).

fragor, -ōris, *m.*, noise, crash, tumult.

frāgrāns, -ntis, fragrant.

frangō, -ere, frēgī, frāctum (3), break, snap (*transitive*).

frāter, -tris, *m.*, brother.

fremō, -ere, -uī, -itum (3), growl, roar ; chafe ; applaud (559).

frēnō, (1), rein, curb, control.

frequēns, -ntis, crowded, in throngs.

fretum, -i, *n.*, strait ; sea

frīgus, -oris, *n.*, cold, chill ; cold fear.

frondeus, -a, -um, leafy.

frōns, -ntis, *f.*, forehead, brow ; cliff-face (166).

frūgēs, -um, *f. pl.*, corn, grain ; produce.

frūstrā, *adv.*, in vain, vainly.

frūstum, -ī, *n.*, piece.

fūcus, -ī, *m.*, drone.

fuga, -ae, *f.*, flight.

fugiō, -ere, fūgī, fly, flee, flee from.

fugō, (1), put to flight, chase ; rout ; scatter.

fulmen, -inis, *n.*, lightning, thunderbolt.

fulvus, -a, -um, yellow, tawny.

fūnāle, -is, *n.*, torch.

fundāmentum, -ī, *n.*, foundation.

fundō, -ere, fūdī, fūsum (3), pour, shed, scatter ; lay low.

fūnus, -eris, *n.*, death.

furiae, -ārum, *f. pl.*, madness, rage.

furō, -ere (3), rage ; boil, seethe (107).

furor, -ōris, *m.*, rage, madness

futūrus, -a, -um, to be, future.

galea, -ae, *f.*, helmet.

gaudeō, -ēre, gavīsus sum (2 *semi-dep.*), rejoice.

gaudium, -ī, *n.*, joy, delight.

gāza, -ae, *f.*, treasure.

geminus, -a, -um, twin, double.

gemitus, -ūs, *m.*, groan, sigh.

gemma, -ae, *f.*, jewel.

gemō, -ere, -uī, -itum (3), groan, sigh, lament.

genetrix, -īcis, *f.*, mother.

genitor, -ōris, *m.*, father.

genitus, -a, -um (*partic. of* gigno), born, sprung.

gēns, gentis, *f.*, race, nation, family, stock (431).

genū, -ūs, *n.*, knee.

genus, -eris, *n.*, race, birth.

germāna, -ae, *f.*, sister.

germānus, -ī, *m* .,brother.

gerō, -ere, gessī, gestum (3), bear, carry, wear ; carry on ; achieve ; bellum gerō, wage war.

gestō, (1), bear, carry.

gīgnō, -ere, genuī, genitum (3), beget, bear (*children*).

glaeba, -ae, *f.*, soil.

glomerō, (1), gather, pile up ; *in pass.*, assemble.

gradior, -ī (3 *dep.*), go, step forth.

gradus, -ūs, *m.*, step.

Grāī, -ōrum, *m. pl.*, Greeks.

grandaevus, -a, -um, aged.

grātēs, *f. pl.*, thanks.

gravis, -e, heavy ; weighty, grave ; authoritative (151) ; pregnant (274).

graviter, *adv.*, strongly, vehemently, grievously.

gremium, -ī, *n.*, bosom.

gressus, -ūs, *m.*, step, steps (401).

gurges, -itis, *m.*, gulf, pool.

gustō, (1), taste.

Gyās (*acc.* Gyan), -ae, *m.*, Gyas (*Trojan hero*).

habēna, -ae, *f.*, rein.

habeō, (2), have, hold.

habilis, -e, fit, convenient ; light (318).

habitus, -ūs, *m.*, dress, guise.

hāc, *adv.*, by this way, here.

haereō, -ēre, haesī, haesum (2), cling ; abide.

hălŏ, (1), am fragrant.

harēna, -ae, *f.*, sand.

Harpalycē, -ēs, *f.*, Harpalyce.

hasta, -ae, *f.*, spear, lance.

hastīle, -is, *n.*, spear-shaft ; lance, spear.

haud, *adv.*, not.

hauriō, -īre, hausī, haustum (4), drink, drain, quaff.

Hebrus, -ī, *m.*, Hebrus.

Hector, -oris, *m.*, Hector.

Hectoreus, -a, -um, of Hector.

Helena, -ae, *f.*, Helen.

herba, -ae, *f.*, grass.

hērōs, -ōis, *m.*, hero.

Hesperia, -ae, *f.*, Italy.

heus!, ho!

hīberna, -ōrum, *n. pl.*, winters.

hībernus, -a, -um, wintry.

hic, haec, hoc, this ; he, she, it ; *pl.*, they.

hīc, *adv.*, here.

hiems, -emis, *f.*, winter ; storm, tempest.

hinc, hence, from here ; then ; hinc atque hinc, on this side and on that (162).

homō, -inis, *m.*, man.

honor, -ōris, *m.*, honour (609), glory, lustre (591) ; service, worship, homage ; offering (49, 736), sacrifice (632) ; reward (253).

horreō, -ēre, -uī (2), shudder, quiver, be fearful ; bristle.

horridus, -a, -um, terrible, dread.

hospes, -itis, *m.*, guest.

hospitium, -ī, *n.*, welcome, hospitality.

hostia, -ae, *f.*, victim, sacrifice.

hostis, -is, *c.*, enemy.

hūc, *adv.*, hither, here.

hūmānus, -a, -um, human, mortal.

humus, -ī, *f.*, ground ; *loc.*, humī, on the ground.

Hyades, -um, *f. pl.*, the Hyades.

hymenaeus, -ī, *m.*, marriage.

iaceō, (2), lie.

iactō, (1), throw, toss about, harass ; utter ; vaunt (140) ; ponder (227).

iaculor, (1 *dep.*), hurl.

iam, *adv.*, now, already ; non iam, no longer.

iamdūdum, *adv.*, long since, for some time past.

ibīdem, *adv.*, in the same place, on the spot, there.

Īdalium, -ī, *n.*, and Īdalia, -ae, *f.*, Idalium *or* Idalia.

īdem, eadem, idem, the same.

ignārus, -a, -um, ignorant, unwitting.

ignāvus, -a, -um, idle, slothful.

ignis, -is, *m.*, fire ; lightning flash (90).

ignōbilis, -e, base.

ignōtus, -a, -um, unknown.

Īlia, -ae, *f.*, Ilia.

Īliacus, -a, -um, Trojan.

Īliades, -um, *f. pl.*, Trojan women.

Īlioneūs (*acc.* Īlionea), -eī, *m.*, Ilioneus.

Īlium, -ī, *n.*, Troy.

Īlius, -a, -um, Trojan.

ille, illa, illud, that ; he, she, it. *pl.*, they.

illīc, *adv.*, there.

Īllyricus, -a, -um, Illyrian.

Īlus, -ī, *m.*, Ilus.

imāgō, -inis, *f.*, image, form, shape ; phantom.

imber, -bris, *m.*, rain ; water.

immānis, -e, huge, vast ; dreadful ; cruel, wicked (616), monstrous.

immineō, -ēre, -uī (2), overhang, threaten, be at hand.

immītis, -e, ruthless, cruel, stern.

immō, *adv.*, nay.

immōtus, -a, -um, motionless, unmoved ; unaltered (257).

impar, -aris, unequal, ill-matched.

impellō, -ere, -pulī, -pulsum (3), drive, push, strike.

imperium, -ī, *n.*, empire, sway ; power (54).

impiger, -gra, -grum, quick, active, speedy.

impius, -a, -um, wicked, impious, unnatural.

impleō, -ēre, -ēvī, -ētum (2), fill.

implicō, -āre, -āvī *or* -uī, -ātum *or* -itum (1), entwine.

impōnō, -ere, -posuī, -positum (3), put on, lay upon.

imprōvīsus, -a, -um, unforeseen, unexpected.

īmus, -a, -um, lowest, bottom of.

in, *prep. with abl.*, in, on ; *with acc.*, into, on to ; against, on.

inānis, -e, empty, void ; unreal.

incautus, -a, -um, unaware, unwary.

incēdō, -ere, -cessī, -cessum (3), move on, step forward.

incendium, -ī, *n.*, fire, conflagration.

incendō, -ere, -endī, -ēnsum (3), kindle ; inflame.

inceptum, -ī, *n.*, enterprise, undertaking ; plan, purpose.

incessus, -ūs, *m.*, step, gait, movement.

incipiō, -ere, -cēpī, -ceptum, begin.

incōgnitus, -a, -um, unknown.

inconcessus, -a, -um, forbidden.

increpitō, (1), chide, urge ; challenge (738).

incubō, -āre, -uī, -itum (3), lie on, brood on.

incultus, -a, -um, untilled, wild.

incumbō, -ere, -cubuī, -cubitum (3), rest, lean, press on ; fall upon (84).

incūsō, (1), chide, accuse ; reproach (410).

incutiō, -ere, -cussī, -cussum (3), strike . . into (*acc. and dat.*).

inde, *adv.*, thence ; then.

indīcō, -ere, -xī, -ctum (3), appoint ; proclaim.

indignor, (1 *dep.*), chafe, be angry.

induō, -ere, -uī, -ūtum (3), put on.

inermis, -e, unarmed.

infandus, -a, -um, unspeakable, dreadful, abominable.

infēlīx, -īcis, hapless, wretched.

inferō, -ferre, -tulī, illātum, bring into, bring against ; me infero, enter.

infīgō, -ere, -xī, -xum (3), pierce ; impale (45).

ingeminō, (1), redouble.

ingemō, -ere, -uī, -itum (3), groan, sigh.

ingēns, -ntis, huge, vast, mighty ; massive (208).

inhumātus, -a, -um, unburied.

inimīcus, -a, -um, hostile ; deadly (123).

iniūria, -ae, *f.*, injury, wrong, injustice, insult.

inlīdō, -ere, -līsī, -līsum (3), dash . . . upon . . . (*acc. and dat.*).

inquam, *defective vb.,* say.

inrigō, (1), infuse (692).

inscius, -a, -um, ignorant, unaware.

inscrībō, -ere, -psī, -ptum (3), scratch on, write on.

insequor, -ī, -secūtus sum (3 *dep.*), follow, ensue ; pursue (241).

insidiae, -ārum, *f. pl.,* wiles, devices ; treachery.

insīdō, -ere, -sēdī, -sessum (3), settle within.

insignis, -e, marked, distinguished ; famous, great (625).

inspīrō, (1), breathe in.

instō, -āre, -stitī (1), press on.

instruō, -ere, -xī, -ctum (3), deck, adorn, furnish.

insula, -ae, *f.,* isle, island.

insuper, *adv.,* above.

intāctus, -a, -um, untouched ; unwed.

intentō, (1), threaten.

inter, *prep. with acc.,* between, among.

interdum, *adv.,* at times.

intereā, *adv.,* meanwhile.

interfor, (1 *dep.*), interrupt.

interior, -ius, inner.

intimus, -a, -um, inmost.

intonō, -āre, -uī (1), thunder.

intrā, *prep. with acc.,* within (455).

intractābilis, -e, stern, stubborn ; formidable, hard to subdue (339).

intrōgredior, -ī, -gressus sum (*dep.*), step into, enter.

intus, *adv.,* within.

invehor, -ī, -vectus sum (*pass. of inveho used as dep.*), drive on.

invīsus, -a, -um, hateful.

invius, -a, -um, trackless, pathless.

Iōpas, m., Iopas.

Iovis, *gen. of* **Iuppiter.**

ipse, -a, -um, -self.

īra, -ae, *f.,* wrath, anger.

is, ea, id, that, *rarely* this ; he, she, it, *pl.* they.

ita, so.

Ītalia, -ae, *f.,* Italy.

Ītalus, -a, -um, Italian.

iter, itineris, n., journey, course.

iubeō, -ēre, iussī, iussum (2), bid, order.

iūdicium, -ī, n., judgment, decision.

iugō, (1), yoke, unite.

iugum, -ī, n., yoke ; ridge, hill.

Iūlius, -ī, m., Julius.

Iūlus (3 *syllables*), **-ī, m.,** Iulus.

iungō, -ere, iūnxī, iūnctum (3), join, unite.

Iūnō, -ōnis, f., Juno.

Iūnōnius, -a, -um, of Juno.

Iuppiter, Iovis, m., Jupiter, Jove.

iūs, iūris, n., right (731), law (426), justice ; ordinance (507).

iussum, -ī, n., command.

iustitia, -ae, f., justice.

iustus, -a, -um, just, fair, right.

iuvenis, -is, m., a youth ; *as adj.,* young.

iuventa, -ae, f., youth (*period of life*).

iuventūs, -ūtis, f., youth (*collective noun*).

iuvō, -āre, iūvī, iūtum (1), help, profit ; please.

Karthāgō, -inis, f., Carthage.

lābor, -ī, lapsus sum (3 *dep.*), slip, glide, glide on ; swoop (394).

labor, -ōris, *m.*, labour, toil ; task ; suffering (460), trouble.
labōrō, (1), work ; broider (639).
lacrima, -ae, *f.*, tear.
lacrimō, (1), weep.
laedō, -ere, laesī, laesum (3), hurt, injure, offend.
laetitia, -ae, *f.*, joy, delight.
laetor, (1 *dep.*), rejoice.
laetus, -a, -um, glad, joyful ; joyous (591).
lapis, -idis, *m.*, stone.
laqueāre, -is, *n.*, panelled *or* fretted ceiling.
largus, -a, -um, large, copious.
lātē, *adv.*, far and wide, widely.
lateō, (2), lie hid, lurk.
latex, -icis, *m.*, liquid ; wine (736).
Latium, -ī, *n.*, Latium.
Lātōna, -ae, *f.*, Latona.
lātus, -a, -um, wide.
latus, -eris, *n.*, side.
laus, laudis, *f.*, praise, fame ; virtue, worth (461).
Lāvīnium, -ī, *n.*, Lavinium.
Lāvīnius, -a, -um, Lavinian.
laxus, -a, -um, loose, slack.
Lēda, -ae, *f.*, Leda.
legō, -ere, lēgī, lectum (3), choose.
lēniō, (4), soften, soothe.
levis, -e, light.
levō, (1), lift ; lighten, relieve.
lēx, lēgis, *f.*, law.
lībō, (1), touch lightly, taste (256) ; pour *or* offer as libation.
Liburnī, -ōrum, *m. pl.*, Liburnians.
Libya, -ae, *f.*, Libya, Africa.
Libycus, -a, -um, Libyan, African.
licet, -ēre, -uit *or* licitum est (2), it is allowed.
līmen, -inis, *n.*, threshold ; door.
linquō, -ere, līquī, (3) leave.

liquēns, -ntis, liquid.
lītus, -oris, *n.*, shore.
locō, (1), place, set.
locus, -ī, *m.*, (*pls.* loci *and* loca) place, spot.
longē, *adv.*, far off, far.
longius, *adv.*, at greater length (262).
longus, -a, -um, long.
loquor, -ī, locūtus sum (3 *dep.*), speak, say.
lōrum, -ī, *n.*, strap ; *pl.*, reins.
luctor, (1 *dep.*), struggle, wrestle.
lūcus, -ī, *m.*, grove.
lūdō, -ere, -sī, -sum (3), play, sport ; beguile, mock, deceive.
lūmen, -inis, *n.*, light ; eye.
lūna, -ae, *f.*, moon.
lūnātus, -a, -um, crescent-shaped.
luō, -ere, -uī (3), loose ; atone for.
lupa, -ae, *f.*, she-wolf.
lūstrō, (1), gaze at, scan ; explore (577) ; move over (608).
lūstrum, -ī, *n.*, age (*properly period of 5 years*).
lūx, lūcis, *f.*, light.
lūxus, -ūs, *m.*, luxury, wealth.
Lyaeus, -a, -um, Bacchic.
lychnus, -ī, *m.*, lamp.
Lycius, -a, -um, Lycian.
Lycus, -ī, *m.*, Lycus.
lympha, -ae, *f.*, water.
lynx, lyncis, *c.*, lynx.

maculōsus, -a, -um, spotted.
maereō, (2), mourn, grieve.
maestus, -a, -um, sad, sorrowful.
māgāle, -is, *n.*, hut.
magis, *adv.*, more.
magister, -trī, *m.*, master, captain, pilot.
magistrātus, -ūs, *m.*, magistrate.

mǎgnanimus, -a, -um, high-souled, noble.

mǎgnus, -a, -um, great ; wide (300).

Maia, -ae, *f.,* Maia.

mǎior, -ius, greater.

malum, -ī, *n.,* evil, trouble.

malus, -a, -um, bad, evil, wicked.

mamma, -ae, *f.,* breast.

maneō, -ēre, mānsī, mānsum (2), remain, abide.

mantǐle, -is, *n.,* towel, napkin.

manus, -ūs, *f.,* hand ; band, troop ; craftsmanship (455).

mare, -is, *n.,* sea.

māter, -tris, *f.,* mother.

mātūrō, (1), hasten.

Māvortius, -a, -um, of Mars ; martial.

māximus, -a, -um, greatest.

mēcum, with me.

meditor, (1 *dep.),* ponder ; purpose, intend.

medius, -a, -um, mid, middle, middle of.

mel, mellis, *n.,* honey.

melior, -ius, better.

melius, *adv.,* better.

membrum, -ī, *n.,* limb.

meminī, -isse, *defective vb.,* remember ; *often with gen.*

Memnōn, -onis, *m.,* Memnon.

memor, -is, mindful, unforgetting.

memorō, (1), tell, relate ; call ; speak (631).

mēns, mentis, *f.,* mind, heart ; intent, plan, purpose.

mēnsa, -ae, *f.,* table ; feast (686).

mēnsis, -is, *m.,* month.

mercor, (1 *dep.),* buy.

meritum, -ī, *n..* desert, service.

merum, -ī, *n..* wine.

mēta, -ae, *f.,* goal, limit.

metuō, -ere, -uī, -ūtum (3), fear.

metus, -ūs, *m.,* fear, terror.

meus, -a, -um, my ; mine.

micō, -āre, -uī (1), flash, flicker.

mīlia, -ium, *n. pl.,* thousands.

mille, *(indeclinable),* a thousand.

minister, -trī, *m.,* attendant, servant.

ministrō, (1), serve ; give, supply ; tend (213).

minor, -us, less ; **minōrēs,** *m. pl.,* descendants (532, 733).

minor, (1 *dep.),* threaten.

minus, *adv.,* less.

mīrābilis, -e, wondrous.

mīrandum, -ī, *n.,* marvel, wonder.

mīror, (1 *dep.),* marvel, wonder at.

mīrus, -a, -um, marvellous, wondrous.

misceō, -ēre, -uī, mixtum *or* **mistum (2),** mix ; trouble (124); confuse, throw into confusion.

miser, -era, -erum, wretched.

miserābilis, -e, pitiful, wretched.

miseror, (1 *dep.),* pity.

mītēscō, -ere (3), grow mild.

mittō, -ere, mīsī, missum (3). send ; dismiss (203).

modo, *adv.,* only.

modus, -ī, *m.,* manner.

moenia, -ium, *n. pl.,* walls.

mōlēs, -is, *f.,* pile, mass ; effort.

mōlior, (4 *dep.),* toil at (564) ; plot, scheme ; build (424) ; wield ; cause (414).

molliō, (4), soften, soothe.

mollis, -e, soft, gentle.

monīle, -is, *n.,* necklace.

mōns, montis, *m.,* mountain.

mōnstrō, (1), show, point out.

mora, -ae, *f.*, delay.,
moror, (1 *dep.*), delay, detain (670).
mors, -tis, *f.*, death.
morsus, -ūs, *m.*, bite.
mortālis, -e, mortal, human.
mōs, mōris, *m.*, custom, manner ;
pl., *often*, character ; de more,
according to custom.
moveō, -ēre, mōvī, mōtum (2),
move, stir, excite ; trouble ;
reveal (262).
mulceō, -ēre, -lsī, -lsum (2),
soothe, assuage.
multum, *adv.*, much.
multus, -a, -um, much ; *pl.*,
many.
mūniō, (4), fortify.
mūnus, -eris, *n.*, gift.
murmur, -is, *n.*, moaning, murmur ; roaring.
mūrus, -ī, *m.*, wall.
Mūsa, -ae, *f.*, Muse.
mūtō, (1), change (*transitive*).
Mycēnae, -ārum, *f. pl.*, Mycene.

nam *or* namque, *conj.*, for.
nāscor, -ī, nātus sum (3 *dep.*), am
born, arise, grow.
nāta, -ae, *f.*, daughter.
nātus, -ī, *m.*, son.
nāvigō, (1), sail ; sail over (67).
nāvis, -is, *f.*, ship.
┝ne, whether ; or.
nē, *conj.*, lest, that not.
nebula, -ae, *f.*, cloud, mist.
nec, neither, nor, and not.
necdum, *adv.*, and not yet.
necnōn, *adv.*, and moreover.
nectar, -aris, *n.*, nectar (*drink of
the gods*).
nectō, -ere, -xuī *or* -xī, -xum (3),
bind, weave.

nefandum, -ī, *n.*, wrong, wicked
ness.
nefandus, -a, -um, wicked, dreadful, horrible.
nemus, -oris, *n.*, grove, wood.
Neptūnus, -ī, *m.*, Neptune.
neque, neither, nor, and not.
nequeō, -īre, nequīvī *or* -iī, am
unable, cannot.
nesciō, (4), am ignorant of.
nescius, -a, -um, ignorant, unwitting.
nexus, -a, -um, *perf. partic. pass.*
of nectō.
nī = nisi, unless.
niger, -gra, -grum, black.
nimbōsus, -a, -um, stormy.
nimbus, -ī, *m.*, cloud, storm.
niteō, (2), shine, glitter.
niveus, -a, -um, snowy.
nō, (1), swim.
nōdus, -ī, *m.*, knot.
nōmen, -inis, *n.*, name.
nōn, *adv.*, not.
nōs, nostrī *or* -trum, we.
noster, -tra, -trum, our ; ours.
nōtus, -a, -um, known, familiar.
Notus, -ī, *m.*, South Wind.
novem, nine.
novitās, -ātis, *f.*, novelty, newness.
novus, -a, -um, new, strange.
nox, noctis, *f.*, night.
noxa, -ae, *f.*, evil deed, harm,
crime ; guilt.
nūbēs, -is, *f.*, cloud.
nūdō, (1), bare, strip ; lay bare,
discover.
nūdus, -a, -um, naked, bare.
nūmen, -inis, *n.*, god, deity ;
power ; majesty ; godhead
(48) ; will (133).
numerus, -ī, *m.*, number.

nunc, *adv.*, now.

nūntiō, (1), tell, announce.

nūtrīmentum, -ī, *n.*, fodder, food ; fuel.

nūtrīx, -īcis, *f.*, nurse.

nympha, -ae, *f.*, nymph.

ō, oh!

ob, *prep. with acc.*, on account of, for the sake of.

obiectus, -ūs, *m.*, jutting out, projection.

obruō, -ere, -uī, -ūtum (3), over-whelm.

obscūrus, -a, -um, dark, hidden.

obstipēscō, -ere, -stipuī (3), am amazed.

obstō, -āre, -stitī (1), resist, oppose : *often with dat.*

obtūnsus, -a, -um, unfeeling, in-sensible.

obtūtus, -ūs, *m.*, gaze.

obvius, -a, -um, meeting, in one's way.

occāsus, -ūs, *m.*, fall.

occubō, (1), fall, lie low.

occulō, -ere, -uī, -cultum (3), hide (*transitive*).

occultus, -a, -um, hidden.

occumbō, -ere, -cubuī, -cubitum (3), fall.

occurrō, -ere, -rrī, -rsum (3), meet.

Ōceanus, -ī, *m.*, Ocean.

oculus, -ī, *m.*, eye.

odium, -ī, *n.*, hatred, ill will.

odor, -ōris, *m.*, odour, fragrance.

Oenotrī, -ōrum, *m. pl.*, Oeno-trians.

offerō, -ferre, obtulī, oblātum, offer, show.

officium, -ī, *n.*, service, kindness.

Oïleus, -ī, *m.*, Oïleus.

ōlim, *adv.*, once, one day.

ollī = illī (*dat. of* ille).

Olympus, -ī, *m.*, heaven, sky.

ōmen, -inis, *n.*, omen, sign.

omnipotēns, -ntis, almighty.

omnis, -e, all, every.

onerō, (1), load.

onus, -eris, *n.*, load, burden.

onustus, -a, -um, laden.

opīmus, -a, -um, rich.

opperior, -īrī, oppertus sum (4 *dep.*), await.

oppetō, -ere, -īvī *or* -iī, -ītum (3), fall, die.

opprimō, -ere, -pressī, -pressum (3), crush, overwhelm.

[ops], opis, *f.*, power ; aid ; *in pl.*, riches, wealth, resources.

optimus, -a, -um, best, excellent.

optō, (1), wish, desire, long for ; choose.

opulentus, -a, -um, wealthy, rich.

opus, operis, *n.*, work.

ōra, -ae, *f.*, shore, coast.

orbis, -is, *m.*, circle ; world ; period.

ordior, -īrī, orsus sum (4 *dep.*), begin.

ordō, -inis, *m.*, order, rank, line ; ex ordine, in order.

Orēas, -adis, *f.*, Oread, mountain nymph.

Oriēns, -ntis, *m.*, the East.

orīgō, -inis, *f.*, origin, birth.

Orīōn, -onis, *m.*, Orion.

orior, -īrī, ortus sum (4 *dep.*), arise ; spring.

ornātus, -ūs, *m.*, garb, adornment.

ōrō, (1), beg, pray, entreat.

Orontēs, -ī, *m.*, Orontes.

ōs, ōris, *n.*, mouth ; face ; lips.

os, ossis, *n.*, bone.

osculum, -ī, *n.*, kiss ; lip.

ostendō, -ere -ndī, -ntum *or* -nsum (3), show ; hold out (206).

ostium, -ī, *n.*, mouth (*of rivers, etc.*).

ostrum, -ī, *n.*, purple.

pābulum, -ī, *n.*, fodder.

paenitet, -ēre, -uit (2 *impers.*) ; me paenitet I repent.

palla, -ae, *f.*, robe.

Pallas, -adis, *f.*, Pallas (*also called* Minerva *and* Athena).

pallidus, -a, -um, pale.

palma, -ae, *f.*, palm ; hand

Paphos, -ī, *f.*, Paphos.

par, paris, equal.

Parcae, -ārum, *f. pl.*, the Fates.

parcō, -ere, pepercī, parsum (3), *often with dat.*, spare, forbear.

parēns, -entis, *c.*, parent ; father, mother.

pāreō, (2), obey (*with dat.*).

Paris, -idis, *m.*, Paris.

pariter, *adv.*, equally, alike ; on equal terms (572).

parō, (1), prepare, make ready.

pars, -rtis, *f.*, part ; side ; some ; share (508).

partior, (4 *dep.*), divide.

partus, -ūs, *m.*, birth.

pāscō, -ere, pāvī, pāstum (3), feed (*transitive*).

pāscor, -ī, pāstus sum (3 *dep.*), feed (*intransitive*), graze.

passus, -a, -um (*partic. of* pandō), spread ; dishevelled (480).

passus, *see* patior.

Patavium, -ī, *n.*, Patavium (= Padua).

pateō, (2), am open ; am revealed.

pater, -tris, *m.*, father.

patera, -ae, *f.*, cup, goblet.

patior, -ī, passus sum (*dep.*), suffer, bear ; allow.

patria, -ae, *f.*, country, fatherland ; home (51).

patrius, -a, -um, father's, native (620).

paucī, -ae, -a, few.

paulātim, *adv.*, little by little.

pāx, pācis, *f.*, peace.

pectus, -oris, *n.*, breast, heart.

pecus, -udis, *f.*, beast, *pl.*, cattle.

pecus, -oris, *n.*, herd.

pēior, -ius, *gen. sg.*, peioris, worse.

pelagus, -ī, *n.*, sea ; flood.

Pelasgī, -ōrum, *m. pl.*, Pelasgi.

pellō, -ere, pepulī, pulsum (3), drive.

pelta, -ae, *f.*, shield.

penātes, -ium, *m. pl.*, household gods ; gods of the larder (704).

pendeō, -ēre, pependī (2), hang.

penetrō, (1), penetrate, reach to ; pierce.

penitus, *adv.*, deeply, far in ; far (200).

Penthesilēa, -ae, *f.*, Penthesilea.

penus, -ūs *or* -ī, *m. or f.*, store ; feast.

peplus, -ī, *m.*, robe.

per, *prep. with acc.*, through , along ; by means of ; upon (214).

peragrō, (1), traverse, wander over.

percutiō, -ere, -cussī, -cussum (3) strike.

perferō, -ferre, -tulī, -lātum, bring, convey, endure, carry on.

perflō, (1), blow through.

Pergama, -ōrum, *n. pl.*, Pergama. (*Troy, or its citadel*).

pergŏ, -ere, -rēxī, -rēctum (3), go on *or* forward, proceed (389).

perīculum, -ī, *n.*, danger.

perlābor, -ī, -lapsus sum (3 *dep.*), glide over.

permisceŏ, -ēre, -uī, -mixtum (2), mingle, mix.

permittŏ, -ere, -mīsī, -missum (3), entrust, permit.

persolvŏ, -ere, -solvī, -solūtum (3), pay.

personŏ, -āre, -uī, -itum (1), sound ; play (741).

**pertemptŏ, (1), thrill, affect deeply (502).

pēs, pedis, *m.*, foot.

pessimus, -a, -um, worst, very bad, very wicked.

pestis, -is, *f.*, plague ; ruin.

petŏ, -ere, -īvī, -ītum (3), seek ; ask ; pursue ; make for (519).

pharetra, -ae, *f.*, quiver.

Phoebus, -ī, *m.*, Phoebus (= Apollo).

Phoenissa, -ae, *f.*, woman of Phoenicia ; Dido (714).

Phoenix, -īcis, *m.*, Phoenician.

Phrygius, -a, -um, Phrygian, Trojan.

Phryx, -ygis, Phrygian.

Phthīa, -ae, *f.*, Phthia.

pictūra, -ae, *f.*, picture, design.

pictus, -a, -um, embroidered (708).

pietās, -ātis, *f.*, piety, goodness.

pingŏ, -ere, -nxī, pictum (3), paint ; embroider.

pinguis, -e, rich, fat.

pius, -a, -um, pious, good, dutiful.

placeŏ, (2), please ; **placet, *perf.* placuit *or* placitum est,** it is resolved.

placidus, -a, -um, calm, serene : undisturbed (249).

placŏ, (1), appease, calm.

plaga, -ae, *f.*, region.

plēnus, -a, -um, full.

plūrimus, -a, -um, most, very many.

plūs, plūris, more.

pluvius, -a, -um, rainy.

pōculum, -ī, *n.*, cup.

poena, -ae, *f.*, penalty, punishment.

Poenus, -ī, *m.*, a Carthaginian.

polliceor, (2 *dep.*), promise.

polus, -ī, *m.*, sky, heaven.

pondus, -eris, *n.*, weight.

pōnŏ, -ere, posuī, positum (3), put, place, set, lay ; lay aside.

pontus, -ī, *m.*, sea.

populŏ, (1), ravage, devastate.

populus, -ī, *m.*, people.

porta, -ae, *f.*, gate.

portŏ, (1), carry.

portus, -ūs, *m.*, harbour

poscŏ, -ere, poposcī (3), ask for.

possum, posse, potuī, am able, can.

post, *adv.*, afterwards ; *prep. with acc.*, after.

posthabeŏ, (2), esteem less.

postquam, *conj.*, when.

potēns, -ntis, powerful.

potentia, -ae, *f.*, power.

potior, (4 *dep.*), seize, get possession of, gain (+ *abl.*).

praecipuē, *adv.*, chiefly.

praeda, -ae, *f.*, prey, booty, spoil.

praemittŏ, -ere, -mīsī, -missum, (3), send on, *or* ahead.

praemium, -ī, *n.*, reward.

praeruptus, -a, -um, sheer, precipitous.

praesēpe, -is, *n.*, dwelling, enclosure (435).

praestāns, -ntis, surpassing, excellent.

praestat, it stands first, it is of more importance (135).

praichtereā, *adv.*, besides, further ; any more.

praevertō, -ere, -rtī, -rsum (3), surprise (721) ; *pass. as dep.*, outstrip (317).

premō, -ere, pressī, pressum (3), press, crush ; tighten (63) ; hide, cover ; chase ; control (54) ; press hard (467).

Priamus, -ī, *m.*, Priam.

prīdem, *adv.*, long ago.

prīmō, *adv.*, at first.

prīmum, *adv.*, first.

prīmus, -a, -um, first ; in primis, chiefly, especially ; prima terra, the edge of the land.

prīnceps, -ipis, *m.*, leader, chief, prince.

prior, -ius, *adv.*, earlier, first.

priusquam, *conj.*, before.

prō, *prep. with abl.*, for, on behalf of ; instead of.

procāx, -ācis, boisterous, stormy (536).

procella, -ae, *f.*, storm, squall.

procerēs, -um, *m. pl.*, chiefs, nobles.

procul, *adv.*, far.

prōdō, -ere, -didī, -ditum (3), betray.

proficīscor, -ī, profectus sum (3 *dep.*), set out, depart.

profor, (1 *dep.*), speak.

profugus, -a, -um, fugitive, exiled.

profundus, -a, -um, deep.

prōgeniēs, -ēī, *f.*, offspring ; breed.

prohibeō, (2), keep away *or* ward off.

prōles, -is, *f.*, offspring.

prōluō, -ere, -uī (3), steep ; se proluere, drink deep (739).

prōmittō, -ere, -mīsī, -missum (3), promise.

prōnus, -a, -um, headlong, face downward.

prope, *adv.*, near ; nearly ; *compar.* propius (526), more closely *or* with more favour.

properō, (1), hasten.

proprius, -a, -um, one's own.

prōra, -ae, *f.*, prow, bow.

prōruptus, -a, -um, bursting forth.

prōspectus, -ūs, *m.*, view.

prōspiciō, -ere, -spēxī, -spectum, look forth ; look forth upon (155) ; see (185).

proximus, -a, -um, nearest, next.

pūbes, -is, *f.*, youth (*collective noun*).

puer, -ī, *m.*, boy.

pūgna, -ae, *f.*, fight.

pulcher, -chra, -chrum, beautiful, fair.

pulsus, *see* pello.

pulvis, -eris, *m.*, dust.

Pūnicus, -a, -um, Carthaginian, Punic.

puppis, -is, *f.*, stern ; *by synecdoche*, ship (69).

pūrgō, (1), clear.

purpureus, -a, -um, bright ; purple ; radiant (591).

Pygmalion, -ōnis, *m.*, Pygmalion.

quā, *adv.*, where ; how ; in any way (682).

quaerō, -ere, -sīvī, -sītum (3), seek, ask ; investigate.

quālis, -e, *relative adj.*, (such) as ;
interrogative adj., what kind of
(752).

quam, *adv.*, how.

quam, *conj.*, than.

quandō, when ; since (*causal*).

quantus, -a, -um, how great ;
(as much) *or* (as great) as.

quārē, *adv.*, wherefore.

quassō, (1), shake, batter ; dis-
able.

quater, four times.

-que, and ; both.

queror, -ī, questus sum (3 *dep.*),
complain, lament.

quī, quae, quod, *rel. pron.*, who,
which, that.

quī, quae, qucd, *interrog. adj.*,
which? what?

quī, quae, quod, *indef. adj.*, any,
some ; ne qua, lest anyhow.

quīcunque, quae-, quod-, *indef.
pron.*, whoever, whatever.

quid, why?

quiēs, -ētis, *f.*, rest, pause ; lull
(723).

quiēscō, -ere, -ēvī, -ētum (3), rest,
am still.

quiētus, -a, -um, calm, tranquil,
quiet, peaceful.

quīn, *adv.*, moreover.

quīnquāginta, fifty.

quippe, *adv.*, doubtless, surely.

Quirīnus, -ī, *m.*, Quirinus(= *Romulus*).

quis, quid, *interrog. pron.*, who?
what?

quis, qua, quid, *indef. pron.*, anyone, anything (*after* si, nisi,
num, ne).

quīs = quibus.

quisquam, quae-, quid- *or* quic-,

indef. pron., anyone, anything
(*in negative sentences*).

quisquis, quidquid *or* quicquid,
indef. pron., whoever, whatever.

quō, *adv.*, whither.

quōcircā, *adv.*, wherefore.

quondam, *adv.*, formerly, once, of
old.

quoque, also, too.

rabiēs, *f.*, rage.

rapidus, -a, -um, swift ; violent,
destructive.

rapiō, -ere, -uī, raptum, seize,
snatch, carry off, ravish.

raptō, (1), carry off, drag away.

raptus, *see* rapio.

rārus, -a, -um, rare, scattered.

ratis, -is, *f.*, ship, bark.

recēns, -ntis, fresh, recent.

recipiō, -ere, -cēpī, -ceptum, take
back, receive ; rescue, save.

reclūdō, -ere, -sī, -sum (3), open,
disclose, reveal.

recondō, -ere, -didī, -ditum (3),
hide.

rēctus, -a, -um, straight, right.

recursō, (1), rush back.

reddō, -ere, -didī, -ditum (3), give
back, restore ; utter (*of words*)
(409).

redoleō, (2), am scented.

redūcō, -ere, -xī, -ctum (3), bring
back.

reductus, -a, -um, withdrawn,
secluded.

redux, -ucis, restored.

referō, -ferre, -tulī, -lātum, take
back ; relate, speak ; answer ;
report (309) ; change (281).

refulgeō, -ēre, -lsī (2), glow; shine.

refūsus, -a, -um (*partic. of* re-
fundo), upheaved.

rēgālis, -e, royal, princely.

rēgīna, -ae, *f.,* queen.

regiō, -ōnis, *f.,* region.

rēgius, -a, -um, royal, princely.

rēgnō, (1), reign, rule.

rēgnum, -ī, *n.,* kingdom, realm ;
rule.

regō, -ere, rēxī, rēctum (3), rule,
guide, sway, control.

reliquiae, -ārum, *f. pl.,* remnant,
remains, leavings.

rēmigium, -ī, *n.,* oarage.

remordeō, -ēre, -rsum (2), sting,
vex, trouble.

removeō, -ēre, -mōvī, -mōtum (2),
remove.

Remus, -ī, *m.,* Remus.

rēmus, -ī, *m.,* oar.

rependō, -ere, -endī, -ēnsum (3),
repay, recompense.

repentē, *adv.,* suddenly.

repetō, -ere, -īvī, -ītum (3), seek,
retrace, trace back.

repōnō, -ere, -posuī, -positum (3),
put away ; bring back, restore.

repostus, -a, -um (=repositus),
hidden away.

requīrō, -ere, -quīsīvī, -quīsītum
(3), seek, long for.

rēs, reī, *f.,* thing, matter ; power,
state ; *pl.,* troubles ; fortunes (452, etc.).

reses, -idis, dormant, slumbering
(722).

resideō, -ēre, -sēdī, -sessum (2),
sit ; recline.

respectō, (1), regard.

respondeō, -ēre, -ondī, -ōnsum (2),
answer ; answer to, agree with
(585).

restō, -āre, -stitī, (1), survive.

resupīnus, -a, -um, fallen back.

resurgō, -ere, -rēxī, -rēctum (3),
rise again.

retegō, -ere, -tēxī, -tēctum (3),
disclose, unfold.

revīsō, -ere (3), revisit, return
to.

revocō, (1), recall, rev.ve.

rēx, rēgis, *m.,* king.

Rhēsus, -ī, *m.,* Rhesus (*a Thracian
prince*).

rīgeō, (2), am stiff.

rīma, -ae, *f.,* chink, gap, crack.

rīpa, -ae, *f.,* bank.

rogitō, (1), question, ask.

Rōma, -ae, *f.,* Rome.

Rōmānus, -a, -um, Roman.

Rōmulus, -ī, *m.,* Romulus.

roseus, -a, -um, rosy.

rota, -ae, *f.,* wheel.

rudēns, -entis, *m.,* rope, cable.

ruīna, -ae, *f.,* downfall, ruin,
wreck, havoc.

ruō, -ere, -ī, -tum (3), *intrans.,*
rush forth (83) ; *trans.,* overthrow ; upheave (85).

rūpēs, -is, *f.,* rock, cliff, crag.

rūs, rūris, *n.,* country, field.

Rutulī, -ōrum, *m. pl.,* the Rutulians.

Sabaeī, -ōrum, *m. pl.,* Sabaeans.

Sabaeus, -a, -um, Sabaean.

sacerdōs, -ōtis, *f.,* priestess.

sacrātus, -a, -um, hallowed, holy.

saeculum, -ī, *n.,* age.

saepe, *adv.,* often.

saepiō, -īre, -psī, -ptum (4), encircle, shroud (411) ; **saeptus,
-a, -um,** veiled (439), girt
(506).

saeviō, (4), rage, grow wild, grow fierce.

saevus, -a, -um, fierce, cruel; stern (138).

sagitta, -ae, f., arrow, shaft.

sāl, salis, m., salt, brine; sea (35), surge.

saltem, adv., at least.

salūs, -ūtis, f., wealth; safety, salvation.

Samos, -I, f., Samos.

sānctus, -a, -um, holy, sacred, reverend (426).

sanguis, -inis, m., blood; stock.

Sarpēdōn, -onis, m., Sarpedon.

sator, -ōris, m., father.

Sāturnius, -a, -um, of Saturn; fem. as noun, Saturnia, (daughter) of Saturn (= Juno).

saxum, -I, n., rock.

scaena, -ae, f., scene; background (164); stage.

scelus, -eris, n., crime; wickedness.

scēptrum, -I, n., sceptre.

scindō, -ere, scidI, scissum (3), cut, divide.

scintilla, -ae, f., spark.

sciō, (4), know.

scopulus, -I, m., rock.

scūtum, -I, n., shield.

Scyllaeus, -a, -um, of Scylla.

sē (sēsē), suI, sibi, sē, reflex. pron., himself, her-, it-, themselves.

sēcessus, -ūs, m., inlet.

sēclūdō, -ere, -sI, -sum (3), shut out, remove.

secō, -āre, -uI, -tum (1), cut.

sēcum, i.e. cum se.

secundus, -a, -um, following; favourable; res secundae, happiness.

sēcūrus, -a, -um carefree, careless.

sed, but.

sedeō, -ēre, sēdI, sessum (2), sit.

sēdēs, -is, f., seat, bed (84); home (205, 247); shrine (681).

sedīle, -is, n., seat.

sēditiō, -ōnis, f., rebellion, mutiny.

sēmita, -ae, f., path.

senātus, -ūs, m., senate.

sententia, -ae, f., opinion, thought, judgment.

sentiō, -Ire, sēnsI, sēnsum (4), feel, perceive; think.

sēnI, -ae, -a, six each; six.

septem, seven.

septimus, -a, -um, seventh.

sequor, -I, secūtus sum (3 dep.), follow.

serēnō, (1), calm, soothe; brighten.

Serestus, -i, m., Serestus (a Trojan hero).

Sergestus, -I, m., Sergestus (a Trojan hero).

seriēs, f., line, row.

sermō, -ōnis, m., talk.

sertum, -I, n., garland, wreath.

servitium, -I, n., slavery.

servō, (1), save, preserve, keep.

seu, whether, or.

sI, if; sI quis, if anyone.

sīc, adv., so, thus.

Sīcania, -ae, f., Sicily.

Siculus, -a, -um, Sicilian.

Sīdon (acc. Sidōna), -ōnis, f., Sidon.

Sīdōnius, -a, -um, Sidonian, Phoenician.

sīdus, -eris, n., star; constellation.

sīgnum, -I, n., sign, device, signet.

silentium, -ī, n., silence.

sileō, (2), am silent.

silex, -icis, m. or f., flint.

silva, -ae, f., wood, forest.

similis, -e, like, similar.

Simoīs, -entis, m., Simois.

simul, adv., at the same time, together; at once (ll. 631, 632).

simulō, (1), pretend, feign.

sīn, conj., but if.

sine, prep. with abl., without.

singulī, -ae, -a, one each; neut., singula, each thing.

sinō, -ere, sīvī, situm (3), allow, permit.

sinus, -ūs, m., bay; fold (of dress).

sīve, see seu.

sociō, (1), associate; give a share in (+ abl.) (600).

socius, -ī, m., comrade.

sōl, sōlis, m., sun.

soleō, -ēre, solitus sum (2 semi-dep.), am accustomed, am wont.

solium, -ī, n., throne.

sōlor, (1 dep.), console; mitigate.

solum, -ī, n., ground, soil.

sōlum, adv., only.

sōlus, -a, -um, alone.

solvō, -ere, solvī, solūtum (3), loosen; do away with; para-lyze (92); free (562).

somnus, -ī, m., sleep.

sonō, -āre, -uī, -itum (1), sound; roar.

sonōrus, -a, -um, loud, echoing.

sōpiō, (4), lull to sleep.

soror, -ōris, f., sister.

sors, -rtis, f., lot.

spargō, -ere -rsī, -rsum (3), scatter.

Spartānus, -a, -um, Spartan.

speculor, (1 dep.), watch.

spēlunca, -ae, f., cavern.

spernō, -ere, sprēvī, sprētum (3), scorn, despise.

spērō, (1), hope.

spēs, -eī, f., hope.

spīrō, (1), breathe.

splendidus, -a, -um, bright, glorious.

spolium, -ī, n., spoils.

sprētus, see spernō.

sponda, -ae, f., couch.

spūma, -ae, f., foam.

spūmō, (1), foam.

stabilis, -e, sure, firm, stable, abiding.

stāgnum, -ī, n., pool; water.

statuō, -ere, -uī, -ūtum (3), set up, build.

sternō, -ere, strāvī, strātum (3), lay low, strike down; spread.

stīpō, (1), press, pack.

stirps, -pis, f., source, stock.

stō, -āre, stetī, statum (1), stand; am fixed, rest on (646).

strāta, -ōrum, n. pl., pavement.

strepitus, -ūs, m., noise, din, tumult.

strīdeō, -ēre (2), creak, hiss, roar; of winds, shriek; of wings, whirr, flap.

strīdor, -ōris, m., creaking, groaning.

stringō, -ere, -nxī, strictum (3), strip, trim.

struō, -ere, -ūxī, -ūctum (3), pile up, arrange.

studium, -ī, n., desire; pursuit, practice.

stupeō, (2), am aghast, am ap-palled.

suādeō, -ēre, -sī, -sum (2), advise, persuade.

sub, *prep.* *with abl.*, under ; towards, about (662).

subdūcō, -ere -xī, -ctum (3), draw up ; *of ships*, beach.

subeō, -īre, -iī, -itum, come under, come close ; enter (171, 400).

subigō, -ere, -ēgī, -āctum (3), subdue, conquer.

subitō, *adv.*, suddenly.

sublīmis, -e, high, lofty.

subnectō, -ere, -xuī, -xum (3), bind beneath.

subnīxus, -a, -um, resting, leaning.

subrīdeō, -ēre, -rīsī, -rīsum (2), smile.

subvolvō, -ere, -lvī, -volūtum (3), roll up (*transitive*).

succēdō, -ere, -cessī, -cessum (3), come under, enter, *with dat.* (627).

succingō, -ere, -nxī, -nctum (3), gird.

succurrō, -ere, -currī, -cursum (3), help, succour (+ *dat.*).

suffūsus, -a, -um, filled, suffused.

sulcus, -ī, *m.*, furrow, trench.

sum, esse, fuī, am.

summergō, -ere, -rsī, -rsum (3), sink (*transitive*), overwhelm, engulf.

summus, -a, -um, highest, greatest, extreme, top of.

super, *prep.* *with acc.*, above, upon ; *with abl.*, above, about (750).

super, *adv.*, further, yet more ; over.

superbia, -ae, *f.*, pride.

superbus, -a, -um, proud.

superēmineō, (2), overtop, surpass.

superī, -ōrum *or* -um, *m. pl.*, those above, the gods.

superō, (1), overcome (537) ; pass (244).

supersum, -esse, -fuī, survive.

supplex, -icis, *m.*, suppliant ; *as adj.*, humble.

suppliciter, *adv.*, in suppliant wise, humbly.

sūra, -ae, *f.*, calf (*of the leg*).

surgō, -ere, -rēxī, -rēctum, (3), rise.

sūs, suis, *c.*, pig, boar, hog.

suscipiō, -ere, -cēpī, -ceptum, catch up, take up, undertake.

suspendō, -ere, -endī, -ēnsum (3), hang (*transitive*).

suspiciō, -ere, -spēxī, -spectum, look up at.

suspīrō, (1), sigh.

suus, -a, -um, *reflex. possessive pron.*, his, her, its, their own.

Sychaeus, -ī, *m.*, Sychaeus (*Dido's late husband*).

syrtis, -is, *f.*, sandbank, shoal, quicksand.

tābeō, (2), am drenched, drip.

tabula, -ae, *f.*, plank, board.

tacitus, -a, -um, silent ; secret (502).

tālis, -e, such.

tam, *adv.*, so.

tamen, *adv.*, nevertheless, yet.

tandem, *adv.*, at length ; *in questions and petitions*, pray.

tangō, -ere, tetigī, tāctum (3), touch.

tantus, -a, -um, so great, as great.

tardus, -a, -um, slow, lingering.

taurīnus, -a, -um, of a bull.

taurus, -ī, m., bull.

tēctum, -ī, n., roof, hall, palace (*especially in pl.*) ; dwelling (425).

tēcum = cum te.

tēgmen, -inis, n., covering, hide.

tellūs, -ūris, f., earth, land.

tēlum, -ī, n., weapon ; spear, sword, dagger.

temnō, -ere (3), scorn, despise.

temperō, (1), calm, control, check.

tempestās, -ātis, f., storm.

templum, -ī, n., temple.

tempus, -oris, n., time.

tendō, -ere, tetendī, tentum *or* tēnsum (3), stretch ; aim, strive ; make one's way (205, 554), bend (*of steps or way*) (410, 656).

teneō, -ere, ūī, tentum (2), hold, possess.

tentō, (1), try.

tentōrium, -ī, n., tent.

tenus, *prep. with abl.*, as far as.

ter, *adv.*, three times.

tergum, -ī, *and* tergus, -oris, n., back, rear ; hide ; ā tergō, from behind.

terminō, (1), end.

ternī, -ae, -a, three each ; three.

terra, -ae, f., earth, land.

terreō, (2), affright, alarm.

tertius, -a, -um, third.

testūdō, -inis, f., tortoise ; dome, vault (*from shape of tortoise shell*) (505).

Teucer, -crī, m., Teucer (*a Greek, brother of Ajax*).

Teucrī, -ōrum *or* -um, m. pl., Teucrians, Trojans.

theātrum, -ī, n., theatre.

thēsaurus, -ī, m., treasure.

Thrēissa, -ae, f., Thracian woman.

thymum, -ī, n., thyme.

Tiberīnus, -a, -um, of the Tiber.

Timāvus, -ī, m., the Timavus.

timor, -ōris, m., fear.

tingō, -ere, -nxī, -nctum (3), dip, plunge.

togātus, -a, -um, that wears the gown.

tollō, -ere, sustulī, sublātum (3), lift, raise ; take away.

tondeō, -ēre, totondī, tōnsum (2), clip, shear.

torqueō, -ēre, torsī, tortum (2), twist, whirl ; hurl (108).

torreō, -ēre, -uī, tostum (2), parch, roast.

torus, -ī, m., couch.

tot, *indeclinable*, so many, as many.

totidem, *indeclinable*, just as many, the same number of.

totiēns, *adv.*, so many times, so often.

tōtus, -a, -um, *gen. and dat.* totius, toti, whole of, all, entire.

trabs, -is, f., beam ; plank (552).

trahō, -ere, trāxī, trāctum (3), draw, drag ; draw out, protract, prolong (748).

trāiciō, -ere, -iēcī, -iectum, pierce.

trānseō, -īre, -iī, -itum, pass over, cross.

trānsferō, -ferre, -tulī, -lātum, transfer, carry across.

trānsfīgō, -ere, -xī, -xum (3), pierce.

tremō, -ere, -uī (3), tremble, quiver.

trēs, -ium, three

tridēns, -ntis, *m.*, trident.
trīgintā, thirty.
Trīnacrius, -a, -um, Sicilian.
Triōnes, -um, *m. pl.*, the Wain (*constellation*).
tristis, -e, sad, sorrowing.
Trītōn, -ōnis, *m.*, Triton.
Trōia, -ae, *f.*, Troy.
Trōiānus, -a, -um, Trojan.
Trōilus, -ī, *m.*, Troilus (*a Trojan*).
Trōius, -a, -um, Trojan.
Trōs, -ōis, *pl.* Trōes, a Trojan.
tū, tuī, *pl.*, vōs, you.
tueor, (2 *dep.*), guard, watch over, protect ; gaze (713).
tulī, *see* ferō.
tum, *adv.*, then.
tumidus, -a, -um, swelling.
tundō, -ere, tutudī, tūnsum (3), beat, strike.
turba, -ae, *f.*, crowd, rabble.
turbō, (1), confuse ; rout ; trouble (515).
turbō, -inis, *m.*, whirlwind ; squall, storm.
tūs, tūris, *n.*, incense.
tūtus, -a, -um, safe ; in tūtum, into safety.
tuus, -a, -um, your, yours.
Tȳdīdēs, -ae, *m.*, son of Tydeus (*Diomedes*).
Typhōius, -a, -um, of Typhoeus.
tyrannus, -ī, *m.*, tyrant.
Tyrius, -a, -um, Tyrian, Phoenician.
Tyrrhēnus, -a, -um, Tuscan, Etruscan.
Tyrus, -ī, *f.*, Tyre.

ūber, -eris, *n.*, richness.
ubi, *adv.*, where, when.
ubique, *adv.*, everywher

ūllus, -a, -um, any.
umbra, -ae, *f.*, shade, gloom.
ūmectō, (1), wet, bedew.
umerus, -ī, *m.*, shoulder.
ūnā, *adv.*, together.
uncus, -a, -um, curved, hooked
unda, -ae, *f.*, wave.
unde, *adv.*, whence.
ūnus, -a, -um, one, alone.
urbs, -is, *f.*, city.
urgeō, -ēre, ursī (2), press, drive, force.
ūrō, -ere, ussī, ustum (3), burn ; vex (662).
usquam, *adv.*, anywhere.
ut *or* utī, *conj.*, *with indic.*, as, when ; *with subj.*, in order that ; how ; that.
utinam, *adv.*, oh that! would that !
ūtor, -ī, ūsus sum (3 *dep.*), use (+ *abl.*)
vacat, (1), there is leisure.
vadum, -ī, *n.*, shallow, shoal ; depth, bottom (126).
validus, -a, -um, strong, stout.
vallis, -is, *f.*, vale, valley.
vānus, -a, -um, vain, false.
varius, -a, -um, various, diverse.
vāstō, (1), lay waste, ravage, destroy.
vāstus, -a, -um, vast ; wild.
-ve, or, either
vēctus, *see* vehō.
vehō, -ere, vēxī, vēctum (3), carry, bear ; *in pass.*, sail (376, *etc.*).
vel, or, either.
vēlāmen, -inis, *n.*, mantle, covering.
vēlivolus, -a, -um, sail-winged, dotted with scudding sails.

vēlum, -ī, *n.*, sail ; covering ; canvas (469).

velut *or* velutī, as if (82) ; as (148).

vēnātrīx, -īcis, *f.*, huntress.

vēndō, -ere, -didī, -ditum (3), sell.

venēnum, -ī, *n.*, poison.

venia, -ae, *f.*, grace, favour ; pardon (519).

veniō, -īre, vēnī, ventum (4), come.

ventus, -ī, *m.*, wind.

Venus, -eris, *f.*, Venus.

verbum, -ī, *n.*, word.

vereor, (2 *dep.*), I fear.

vērō, *adv.*, in truth, indeed.

verrō, -ere, (3), sweep, sweep away.

versō, (1), turn ; ponder, plan.

vertex, -icis, *m.*, head, top ; eddy, whirlpool, vortex ; gulf.

vertō, -ere, -tī, -sum (3), turn, change ; overturn, overthrow.

verū, -ūs, *n.*, spit, skewer.

vērus, -a, -um, true.

vescor, -ī (3 *dep.*), feed on (+ *abl.*).

Vesper, -eris, *m.*, evening, the Evening Star.

Vesta, -ae, *f.*, Vesta.

vester, -tra, -trum, your, yours.

vestis, -is, *f.*, robe, garb, raiment.

vetō, -āre, -uī, -itum (1), forbid.

vetus, -eris, old.

via, -ae, *f.*, way ; journey ; street (422).

vīcī, *see* vinco.

victor, -ōris, *m.*, conqueror ; *as adj.*, triumphant.

vīctus, *see* vinco.

vīctus, -ūs, *m.*, food ; living

videō, -ēre, vīdī, vīsum (2), see ; *in pass.*, *very often*, seem.

vīgintī, twenty.

villus, -ī, *m.*, nap (*of cloth*).

vinciō, -īre, vinxī, vinctum (4), bind.

vincō, -ere, vīcī, vīctum (3), conquer, overcome, defeat.

vinculum *or* vinclum, -ī, *n.*, bond, fetter, chain ; cable (168).

vīnum, -ī, *n.*, wine.

vir, -ī, *m.*, man (*gen. pl. sometimes* virum).

vīrēs, *see* vīs.

virgō, -inis, *f.*, maiden.

virtūs, -ūtis, *f.*, valour ; virtue.

vīs, *acc.* vim, *abl.* vī, *f.*, force, violence, strength ; *pl.* vīrēs, -ium, strength, power.

vīscera, -um, *n. pl.*, flesh, meat

vīta, -ae, *f.*, life.

vītālis, -e, of life.

vīvō, -ere, vīxī, (3), live.

vīvus, -a, -um, alive, living.

vix, *adv.*, scarcely.

vocō, (1), call, summon ; invoke (290).

volō, (1), fly.

volō, velle, voluī, am willing, wish.

volucer, -cris, -cre, swift.

volūtō, (1), roll (725), revolve, brood on, meditate.

volvendus, -a, -um, rolling.

volvō, -ere, volvī, volūtum (3), roll ; pass, traverse ; tend ; unroll (262) ; ponder (305).

vorō, (1), devour, engulf.

vōs, *pl.*, you.

vōsmet, *emphatic form of above*, you yourselves.

vōtum, -ī, *n.*, vow, prayer.

vōx, vōcis, *f.*, voice ; word.

vulgō, (1), make known, noise abroad.

vulgus, -ī, *n.*, common people, common herd.

vulnus, -eris, *n.*, wound, hurt.

vultus, -ūs, *m.*, face, countenance ; glance.

Xanthus, -ī, *m.*, Xanthus.

Zephyrus, -ī, *m.*, the West Wind.